Women of Spirit
Transforming Lives

Compiled and Edited by
"Twinkle" Marie Manning

Women of Spirit, Transforming Lives
is the second volume in this Matrika Press series.

Contributors include:

Anne B. Gass
Anya Searle
Arica Walters
Beth Amine
Carole Fontaine
Cheryl Partridge
Danielle Dufour
Deana Sanderson
Erin Colene
Fatima Al-Sayed
Jaishree Dow-Spielman
Jane Sloven
Kiana Love
Leana Kriel
Melissa Kennedy
Mika Leone
Pam Swing
Patricia Diorio
Sloane Reali
Tam Veilleux

Women
of
Spirit

Transforming Lives

Compiled and Edited by
"Twinkle" Marie Manning

Matrika Press

"The knowledge that you have emerged wiser
and stronger from setbacks means that you are,
ever after, secure in your ability to survive.
You will never truly know yourself, or the strength
of your relationships, until both have been tested
by adversity. Such knowledge is a true gift, for all
that it is painfully won, and it has been worth more
than any qualification I ever earned."

— J.K. Rowling

Dedication

For Suu Feathers,
Shiloh Sophia,
Sue Hoya Sellars
and Lenore Thomas Straus.

A lineage of artists and storytellers
for which I am ever blessed to be a part.

"Twinkle" Marie Manning

To the Wise Women of old, and to the future Wise
Women we pass Our wisdom to, thank you for
keeping the Circle alive.

In love and trust from the
Women of Spirit Contributors

ISBN: 978-1-946088-57-4 (Print)
ISBN: 978-1-946088-58-1 (eBook)

Library of Congress Control Number: 2021951889

1.Spirituality 2.Sacred Feminine 3.Self-Exploration 4.Philosophy
5.Healing 6.Creativity 7.Title

Matrika Press
P.O. Box 115
Rockwood, Maine 04478
Editor@MatrikaPress.com

Matrika Press

www.MatrikaPress.com

First Edition
Printed in the USA

Front cover art by: "Twinkle" Marie Manning
Back cover photo by: MooseheadLakeRetreats.org

TABLE OF CONTENTS

Preface

The freedom to share our joys, triumphs and metamorphoses, as well as vulnerably and bravely disclosing betrayals, sorrows and griefs, are valuable narratives women around the globe continually seek to discover. Sourcing and imparting universal wisdoms. Distilling truths. Processing our human experiences, in particular the ability for women to tell our own stories, from our own perspectives and with the intention of helping others, can be a source of healing - for author and reader. The *Women of Spirit* anthology series was created with that in mind.

This is the second *Women of Spirit* volume. Its theme: *Transforming Lives*. Our contributors come from many parts of the globe, with diverse backgrounds and have shared in a variety of ways. Some authors have shared from the vantage of their personal stories of transformation, as well as those of historical heroines, and some have presented their materials in a how-to style, offering step-by-step models from within their arena of teaching and expertise.

Women of Spirit: Transforming Lives contains essays, articles, advice-columns, blogs and excerpts from within contributing authors' books. Also included are poems, rituals, prayers, meditations, mantras, photographs and art. The spelling choices of words have been kept in alignment with the author's country of origin. The spacing style throughout is, with intention, more pronounced than a typical manuscript, so as to help facilitate contemplative reading.

The cover features art I created under the guidance of my dear friend Suu Feathers. The style and process of painting is in the lineage taught to her by Shiloh Sophia, herself a renaissance woman who communicates her philosophy through painting, storytelling and illustrations. This book is dedicated to them and to their artistic foremothers: Sue Hoya Sellars and Lenore Thomas Straus who promoted the ideals of 'Intentional Creativity' - which has been adopted as a spiritual principle of many artists and writers alike, including me.

The manifestation of my own creativity is derived from my awe of Nature and of the Ethereal, in equal proportions. The motivation for creating, be it writing or painting, often stems from the mystery and the mysterious. Yet, the discipline is resolutely from embodying my physical place in the world.

Over the years I have produced all manner of media and have held the titles of: Television Producer, Radio Host, Event Facilitator, Retreat Leader,

Interfaith Minister, Development Director, Magazine Editor and Columnist, Published Author, Published Poet, Book Editor and Book Publisher are among the ones that continually weave together throughout my life. Often they overlap one to the other and the next. For the *Women of Spirit* anthology series I am the Curator, and what a blessing it is!

This collection of authors each offer unique glimpses of transformation and healing. Each brings with them wisdom it is my absolute honor to share with the world. Our hope is that you find what is contained within this book is inspiring, and we invite you to embrace the parts that resonate with you on your transformational journey.

May it be so.

"Twinkle" Marie Manning

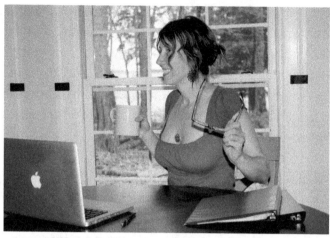

"Twinkle" Marie Manning is a seasoned writer and poet. In addition to her own books, Twinkle's work has been published in several Poetry Anthologies (Florida) and she also had columns in Island Life Magazine (Florida), Island Voice Magazine (Florida), Colonial Times (Massachusetts) and she was included in LifeByMe. Featured stories about Twinkle have appeared in The MONTECITO MESSENGER, Concord Journal, Rolling Thunder, Bangor Daily, Portland Press and other local presses. She is an interfaith minister, liturgist and retreat leader, as well as an award winning television producer, development director and event planner. While she considers herself semi-retired in the television arena, she continues her role as executive producer of the *Empowering Women* television series and signature events, as well as consulting with stations and producers on projects. Twinkle is the founder of *TV for Your Soul* and *Moosehead Lake Retreats*.

www.TwinklesPlace.org
www.EmpoweringWomenTV.org
www.TVforYourSoul.org
www.MooseheadLakeRetreats.org

"Twinkle" painting in California - Autumn 2014:

"Twinkle" painting and sketching in Maine - Autumn 2018:

"Twinkle" painting on Kineo - Summer 2020:

"Twinkle" painting in Maine - Autumn 2020:

Contributors

Anne B. Gass

Activist. Author. Historian.

Anne B. Gass developed her passion for women's rights history while writing a book about her amazing activist great-grandmother; *Voting Down the Rose: Florence Brooks Whitehouse and Maine's Fight for Woman Suffrage*. In 2015 the research for her next book led Anne on a cross-country journey, retracing the route intrepid suffrage activists had taken a century before to demand voting rights for women from Congress and the President. The result was *We Demand: The Suffrage Road Trip*, a historical novel published in 2021. Anne draws strength from all the women who fought so long and hard for equality, and loves finding and telling the stories of courageous women forgotten by history. She speaks frequently on her research in hopes of inspiring others to continue the struggle. She currently serves on Maine's Permanent Commission on the Status of Women and as Vice-Chair of the Gray Town Council.

www.AnneBGass.com

We Demand
The Suffrage Road Trip

No one gave women the right to vote. They had to fight for it; over and over and over again. The right to vote remains the only one women have that is protected by the US Constitution, because, at this moment, the Equal Rights Amendment has not been ratified. All of our other rights have been won through laws, legal opinions, and executive orders. These are fragile and easily undone, so the fight for equality – and for control over our bodies - continues today.

We Demand: The Suffrage Road Trip is just one example of women's extraordinary battle for voting rights. A historical novel, *We Demand* is based on an actual trip that took place in 1915, when four women left San Francisco for Washington DC on a desperate and dangerous mission to demand an amendment to the US Constitution enfranchising women.

The story unfolds through the eyes of Ingeborg Kindstedt and Maria Kindberg, middle-aged lesbians and Swedish immigrants who own the car, do all the driving, and fix what goes wrong. The roads are terrible, and the weather is worse. They lose their way in a trackless Nevada desert and get stuck in the mud in Kansas, among many other adventures. Ingeborg was the mechanic, while Maria did all the driving.

I fell in love with Ingeborg and Maria when I retraced their route in 2015, and was astonished to find they'd gotten so little recognition for all they did. It was likely because they spoke accented English, and didn't fit the profile of the young, well-educated, modern American-born woman that suffrage leaders were trying to promote.

We Demand is a thoroughly researched tribute to Ingeborg and Maria, and to the grit and determination of the suffrage movement that launched the trip. Humorous and nail biting by turns, it seamlessly joins this rich history with an unflinching look at the issues that swirled in and around the suffrage movement; racism, classism, misogyny, and xenophobia.

The excerpt below is of one of the exciting moments of their trip. While I had to imagine the details, this is based on an actual event - crossing a pass in a blizzard from Laramie to Cheyenne. They were the only ones to make it over the pass that day. (Emilie is their car, named after a Swedish suffragist, Emilie Rathou.)

Soon they were under way again, creeping forward cautiously. Emilie seemed to want to charge down to Cheyenne like a horse returning to the barn, and Maria had to work the brake, especially in the steeper sections. There were frightening moments when Emilie simply slid on her own, heedless of the brake or the steering wheel. The snow and wind once again lashed the car and obscured the terrain on either side of the road, and Ingeborg tried not to think about disappearing over some unseen cliff. Sometimes Emilie yawed sideways like a half-broken horse before coming to rest, and then Maria had to coax her into pointing her nose back downhill. This went on for some time until the road leveled out a little and they could all catch their breath. Maria's eyes were wide and staring, her hands locked on the steering wheel, and Ingeborg thought she could see her friend trembling beneath her heavy coat.

They crept forward, and suddenly Maria brought the car to a stop. "Look ahead," she said hoarsely. "Too steep."

Ingeborg grabbed the cloth and wiped away at the windshield, and they squinted out over Emilie's bonnet. The road simply disappeared into the storm. Ingeborg pried open her door and got out to look. The snow was over her boot tops and the wind whipped her skirts; she just managed to grab her hat before it whirled off her head. She stepped forward carefully to peer over the hill, and her heart stopped. Maria was right. The road dropped steeply for several hundred feet before curving around to the right and disappearing into a tunnel of falling snow. Even if they could make it down the first steep section she had no idea how they'd make the turn once the car started sliding, as it surely

would, or what they'd hit at the bottom. The cold pressed in on her, sending icy fingers down the back of her neck, and she knew they couldn't wait until the storm cleared. They had to keep going.

She looked around and off to her right saw a thick pine, its gnarled bark coated with snow. If she tied the rope to the car, then wrapped it around the tree, she and Sara could pay it out to slow the car's descent, at least partway down the hill. She trudged back to the boot and got the rope out, shaking out the loops. She could see right away that it wasn't nearly long enough, maybe thirty feet or so. She put the rope back.

They'd have to ride it down as best they could. She yanked open the passenger door and climbed back into the car, bringing with her a blast of wind and fresh snow. "It's steep," she said, "but we can't stay here. We'll freeze." She turned and looked at Maria, and said with more confidence than she felt, "The snow's deep, and it's drifted into a bank down at the bottom, on your side of the road. Then it curves to the right, and I can't see after that. If we start over on the left here and go down as slow as we can, maybe you can gun it around the turn when we get near the bottom. If not, we'll slide into the bank and have to dig out. Either way, we'll manage. You ready?"

Maria nodded, and backed up several feet so she could maneuver over to the left side of the hill. They could just make out a Lincoln Highway marker poking out of the snow halfway down, suggesting the outlines of the road. She inched the car forward. Gas, brake. Gas, brake, until the car was fully over the crest of the hill and began to slide. Maria's face was pale, and her foot rode the brake so hard she was half rising out of her seat. Emilie began sliding to the left so Marie cranked the steering wheel to the right, the car overcorrecting and sliding almost sideways down the slope. Ingeborg wondered briefly if the wheels would pop off but that thought quickly left her as the car nosed into a snowbank on the righthand side and then spun fully around so they were sliding backward down the hill, gaining speed.

Maria worked the brakes and the steering wheel to no avail, and the sides of the road were sliding past them at a frightening rate. Time seemed to slow down and the storm outside was forgotten. Sara let out a little moan, and Ingeborg looked around frantically to see what they might hit. Just as she noticed that they seemed to be sliding more to one side, the car's left rear wheel became lodged in a snowdrift and they thunked almost to a stop. Maria steered to the right and got her foot back on the gas, spinning the wheels until the weight of the

engine pulled the car around and the nose was once again pointing downhill. This was better, but they were still sliding; again they picked up speed and the curve at the bottom of the hill was approaching quickly.

"Get ready!" Ingeborg gasped to Maria, and then, a few seconds later, "Now!"

Anya Searle

Energy Healer. Rose Priestess. Entrepreneur.

Anya Searle, the Creator of Radiant Goddess Temple, is an Intuitive Energy Healer, Rose Priestess, and Occupational Therapist. She passionately helps women to reconnect to a radiant goddess within and embody sacred feminine essence and sovereignty. As an intuitive energy healer, Anya helps women to achieve a state of balance and well-being by uncovering subconscious limiting belief systems, conditioning, healing trauma and unresolved emotions, and past life influences. Anya is devoted to serving women to unleash their true feminine power and embody their highest alignment and true divine self-expression.

www.RadiantGoddessTemple.com

My Journey
to Discover Divine Purpose

January 30th of 2015, I was invited by a friend to a book signing. Despite not knowing what the book was about, I was consumed by excitement. I was in the thick of going through a spiritual awakening and was hungry to connect with inspiring people who could further propel me on my spiritual journey and feed my soul.

My awakening began on my honeymoon in Mexico in June of 2014. I remember visiting the sacred sites of Chichen Itza and Mayan Villages. I did not know at that time how being there would activate me and transform my life. On my flight back to the US, my husband asked me about what was next for our relationship. He wanted to know if I was ready to start a family and I simply responded that I wanted to focus on my spiritual growth.

Since our trip to Mexico, I started to experience one synchronicity after another leading me towards self-discovery and a deeper connection with Spirit. I began communicating with Angels. My husband started to question my sanity. As I started to drift away from him, I noticed I was no longer resonating with some patterns in life, and some relationships no longer seemed meaningful.

I began to rely on my intuition and connection to Source. My spiritual development was important to me and consuming most of my time. My friend introduced me to the energy healing modality BodyTalk that opened me up furthermore. I started to see the world as a multi-dimensional quantum field of possibilities. I was excelling at connecting with that field and taking charge of my life. I was on the path of becoming a BodyTalk practitioner and was excited to do energy healing full time.

My life at the time was unfolding magically. I remember one day listening to Gabby Bernstein who guided this amazing meditation at the Wanderlust festival. She called it a miracle meditation and I was so excited to experience it. However, little did I know that it was going to create a miracle in my life. Gabby guided us to connect to our inner joy, and I immediately felt this overwhelming feeling of joy of being pregnant. My whole body started to tingle with excitement as I was chanting the mantra:
"Ek Ong Kar Sat Our Prasad Sat Our Prasad Ek Ong Kar."
Two months later, I found out I was pregnant. I later recommended this meditation to all my friends looking for miracles.

The pregnancy allowed me to continue my spiritual path; however, I was reminded daily of the importance of being present in my body and honor my time as a SPIRITUAL being having a HUMAN experience. All I wanted to do at that time was to

connect to Spirit. I was escaping my physical body in hour-long meditations. Becoming a mother allowed me to reconnect to myself in a much deeper way.

Becoming a mother was a magical experience. My connection to my husband strengthened through this experience and we were excited for our new life together. Yet, soon after my daughter's birth it all started to fall apart. My husband lost his job, and financial stress became overbearing. He injured his back and was no longer able to work or complete simple daily tasks. I felt overwhelmed by responsibilities and we were drowning in credit card debt. Our fighting became a norm, and we were no longer connecting as partners. I felt stuck, unhappy, and lost. Until one day, I was diagnosed with Multiple Sclerosis, a chronic and debilitating condition. I was in complete shock and had a difficult time accepting my new reality. I knew my life had to change drastically, and I made a difficult decision to separate from my husband. We grew so far apart that nothing could bring us close together again.

During our difficult separation, being newly diagnosed with Multiple Sclerosis, and drowning with debt, I was scared yet empowered to turn my life around. One night I was journaling, and all I wanted to do was complain WHY ME? As I was indulging in my sorrows and victimhood, I heard the voice saying that my challenges are here to serve me and become the most powerful catalyst in my life for healing and inner growth. I felt a sense of relief and empowerment at that moment, and I carry this feeling to help me get through any challenges in life.

It is here to help me! It is here to serve me. It is here to heal and transform me, and I am honored and grateful for the strength and resilience I am building with each challenge in my life.

After getting back on my feet and healing my marital wounds, I was ready to date again. I've done a lot of inner work and was ready to attract the perfect partner. I knew my worth and had set strong standards for anyone entering my and my daughter's life. I was wounded yet strong. I had my Spirit ally to count on for the guidance I needed. I opened myself up and was ready to receive.

After trying online dating for a month, I knew it was not for me. As I was going to end my journey online, I received a message that grabbed my attention. It was not a "hey beautiful" or "what are you doing tonight" kind of message. It was from a man who openly shared his story, what he was looking for, and how we would make a great match based on our compatibility. I decided to give him a chance. The same day we started to message each other back and forth and I felt this overwhelming sensation in my chest. I felt this massive heart expansion, like my heart was cracking open. I knew our connection was special and was eager to explore this possibility.

We met two days later. I knew right away we had lifetimes together. The connection grew at a

lightning speed. I was excited to be with someone who truly understood me and shared many of the same beliefs and desires for the future. He was charming, open, communicative, and super vulnerable. I was completely in!

Soon after, I knew something was off. It slowly discovered that he was going through a very challenging time and was using drugs to numb the pain and escape reality. Having a previous history with partners who used drugs, I knew I had to end it. I was afraid it was going to negatively impact my health and relationship with my daughter. Every time I ended the relationship, I was completely devastated and instantly felt a magnetizing pull back to him. My mind was telling me to stay away, and my heart would not let go. I was open to holding space for him to rise above his addiction. We did this dance for one year. I so desperately wanted for it to work; however, it was not in my control. I've started to look inside to understand why I was attracting partners with addiction and what that meant. I knew the lesson would continue repeating itself until I took responsibility for my inner reality. I remember the only thing that could bring me peace is doing *Ho'Oponopono* mantra every time he would go "offline." I could feel his every emotion and could not understand why we were so connected yet could not be in a healthy relationship.

I finally had to end it. I was devastated. My partner moved to Austin, Texas where he was going to rehab. During this time, we stayed connected. Our desire

to be together allowed us to be completely open and vulnerable with each other. We both agreed to hold space for each other to show up with our darkest truths and mirror back the light we needed in each other to be witnessed, transformed, and healed. We started to connect every morning by synchronizing our breaths through breathing exercises, setting intentions for the day, and sharing our written commitments to honor our sacred union. Although we could not physically connect for six months, we felt a strong spiritual connection that we could not explain until I began to receive messages from Spirit that I was in a Twin Flame relationship.

We both were new to the Twin Flame paradigm; however, it just felt like truth to us, so we leaned into it. We were able to understand the different stages of the Twin Flame relationship and resonated with each stage. We knew that the separation stage was part of the process, and we were eager to work on ourselves to allow the reunion to happen.

The reunion stage of our relationship continued to be challenging yet rewarding at the same time. I would say it's not for everyone. Imagine your partner triggering and bringing your awareness to the deepest wounds, traumas, and belief systems on the daily! It's like doing shadow work non-stop! It can become very intense, overwhelming, and impossible to have a healthy relationship. Yet, I look at it as part of my spiritual journey and process of deepening my healing and growth. In the end, it's worth it because the

connection is nothing like I've experienced before.

The biggest gift my partner has given me was the ability to step into my greatness. He was able to tap into my full potential and remind me of my magnificence. I had to let go of my fears to fully step into my spiritual work.

I learned through my pain that everything is here to serve me on my highest evolution. I learned to take ownership of my wounds, traumas and limiting belief systems to allow healing and transformation to happen. I disconnected from my diagnosis and began to see myself as a healthy and radiant being.

Through my darkest moments of self-discovery, I witnessed the most beautiful inner child that needed my attention. As my healing journey continued, I began to reconnect to my sacred feminine and masculine essence. The Sacred Feminine started to guide me and inspire me to serve other women. Today, I am proudly helping women reconnect to their inner goddess, heal, and integrate passion and pleasure into their journey.

Who would have known six years ago, on the way to the book signing, that I would be honored to be featured in the second edition of the *Women of Spirit* book?

Arica Walters

Life-Coach. Spiritual-Teacher. Peace-Warrior.

Arica loves to help and support people in their journey for healing & self-mastery. She is very passionate about her work and truly believe in everyone's potential and ability to co-create a life they choose to live. Arica holds a Master's Degree in Metaphysical Science and Practitioner Diploma from the University of Metaphysics. Founder of Namaha Retreat Limited in New Zealand and was also an Executive Director (Corporate Strategy) in a public listed company in Singapore, she is also a successful businesswoman, a wife, a mother, coach & healer. Her works include Coaching & Counselling, Lucia Light Experience, Hypnotherapy, Ancestral Healing, Spiritual Teaching and Meditation. She is also a co-author for the book *Walking with Masters*. Arica is currently studying Doctoral Degree in Theocentric Psychology & Ph.D specialising in Relationship Dynamics.

www.AricaWalters.com

Freedom
from Sufferings through Peace

Everything in this world is made of vibrations that vibrate within a frequency range that our physical senses can detect. In reality, our material universe is made from spiritual light, the primal energy from our Creator that has been lowered in vibration to a specific spectrum of frequencies. As the spiritual light is lowered in vibration, it first enters the highest range of the material realm known as Identity Realm (also known as Etheric Realm), taking on a particular form. As it flows through the next level (Mental Realm and Emotional Realm), the light takes on a denser form until it finally takes on the densest form, which our physical senses can detect.

These four levels of Material Universe also correspond to our four lower bodies (Identity Body, Mental Body, Emotional Body and Physical Body). When we move from the physical realm into the subsequent division, we enter the realm of feeling. Above that is the realm of thought, and above that is the realm of identity. Many religions and philosophies, such as Buddhism, Greeks, and other esoteric teachings, described these four realms as the Earth's four corners. Thus, they were called Earth, Water, Air and Fire. This concept also corresponds to the ancient idea of squaring of the circle, where the circle represents Heaven or Ether, and it is infinite

and undivided in terms of time and space. The square represents Earth, or the material universe, which is the realm of space and time. It is created by taking the infinite realm of the circle and dividing it into four directions, four dimensions, that manifest as the coordinates of time and space.

On a personal level, the energy flows from our spiritual self through the layers of the subconscious mind until it reaches the conscious mind. The energy flows from the realm of spirit, and it first enters our identity body, which is the part of our mind that stores the memories of our experiences in the material world. It also keeps the sense of identity built through our soul's journey over many lifetimes. When the primary life energy first enters our mind or being, it flows through our sense of identity and is therefore coloured by our sense of identity. It includes how we see the world, how we see God and our relationship to the world and God. It is, therefore, the foundation for how we respond to life in this realm.

As the energy flows through our identity body, it enters our mental body, the realm of thought. In this realm, the energy is coloured by our beliefs about ourselves and the world. Our sense of identity determines our thoughts, and they can be adapted to or influenced by specific situations we encounter in this world. In other words, our sense of identity determines how we see the big picture, whereas our thoughts relate to how we understand the details of that picture. Our sense of identity determines how we

see the world, and our thoughts determine how we think the world works.

After the energy flows through the thought body, it enters the realm of feeling. This is our emotional body, where it contains our feelings about ourselves and the world. Emotions are simply energy in motion, and the energy does not have any sense of right or wrong. They are the forerunners for physical action. So our emotions determine how we act upon thoughts. Thought itself cannot lead to action. It is simply an idea. And for the idea to be translated into physical activity, the thought must have direction and intensity added by an emotion. Our emotions will direct our thoughts into a specific action, and the intensity of our emotions will determine the power of the action.

The final step is that the energy enters the physical brain and nervous system when our emotions are translated into actions. The actions will be determined by the direction and the intensity of the feelings behind them. But, of course, the direction and intensity of the emotion are also determined by the thought, and the thought is determined by our sense of identity and our worldview.

As we understand how energy works, we need to transfer this understanding to the material universe as a whole and see how our world works. The material universe has the same four different octaves or levels, four different bodies. They correspond to the four levels of our mind because, indeed, the Universe is

simply the mind of God. The material Universe is created from our Creator's primal energy, which flows through the identity, thought and feeling realms until it manifests in the matter realm.

When we look at this basic flow of energy through the four levels of the material Universe, we can also begin to understand that the level of matter results from hidden causes that take place at the three higher levels of the emotion, the thought, and the identity bodies. Thus, what we are seeing in this world now, is simply a projection of the images found in the three higher levels of the collective consciousness.

As we contemplate this concept, we can also realise that the matter realm is the effect while the three higher levels are the cause. Therefore, if we want to change our outer circumstances, we must begin by changing our feelings, thoughts, and sense of identity. Only when we change the images found in the three higher bodies will we change those that appear in the matter world. Likewise, on a planetary scale, the key to removing human suffering is to purify the emotional, thought and the identity body of the planet.

On our planet Earth currently, we are seeing so many imperfect manifestations and so much human suffering because the three higher bodies of humankind have been polluted by a flawed sense of identity, thoughts, and impure emotions. It happened when humanity fell into a lower state of consciousness, which also led to the current imperfect conditions in

human suffering, natural disasters and many other calamities. And this is the actual cause of suffering.

So how do we break free from all those suffering and start creating the Golden Age on Earth?

First is to understanding how our consciousness fell, and start walking the path of self- mastery for inner peace, so that we gradually let go of the limited belief system and the separate selves that caused the fall. We have to surrender all ego that continues to trick us into believing that we can be at peace only when certain external conditions are met. We know that the external conditions are nothing but the reflection of our inner states. We will only have conditions of peace in our life and on our planet when we decide to be at peace inside ourselves, regardless of the external conditions.

And as spiritual beings or lightworkers, the greatest service for eradicating human suffering, conflict and war from this planet is to commit ourselves to walk the inner Path of Peace. True service is what raises the Earth above the dualistic state of consciousness. To give this kind of service, we must be at peace within ourselves.

The following message has been channelled to me for the Group Meditation for World Peace that I conducted, and I would love to share with you here.

"The power of peace lies within. It is the state of being that already exists. It is up to you to see it, and as you see it, you project it into or onto the world. The current world is the projection of the collective consciousness. It is an out-picturing of the collective's identity, thoughts, emotions and actions. Therefore, it is at exactly where it is supposed to be at this moment. For if you can see in God's eyes, where there is no right and wrong, and there is no good and evil, you will see that everything that happened or is happening is still part of the purpose of the whole Creation.

Yet behind what you see in the world now that is less than perfect is an immaculate conception of a beautiful world that the 7 Elohims had created Earth to be. It is still here, and it is up to you to see. It is only temporarily veiled by the ignorance caused by the illusion of separation. Lift that veil and uncover the beautiful world, the Golden Age on Earth. See it with your Higher Self's eyes. See it with God's eyes. See the beauty of love, peace and joy. Live in this world. Project your vision into our surroundings, your cities, your states, country and the world. You alone have the power to create the world that you are now seeing.

See people hugging and embracing one another, see lovers hand in hand. See the children playing and laughing. See the people of all races, religions, nationalities, genders and cultures, and animosity coming together in love and peace. See the government, the politicians, police men and all other government servants working with the people with one common goal. The goal of creating unity and Oneness, in love and peace. See the soldiers and fighters putting down their weapons and instead choosing love and peace. Feel the joy and abundance of resources that are more than enough for every person on Earth to have a life of good health and wealth. In this world, there is no judgement, no hatred, no fear, no scarcity, no discrimination, no sufferings, no rage, no inequality, no competition, no pollutions, no diseases and no separation. There is only beauty, abundance, Love, Peace, Freedom and Oneness.

Walk with God in this world. You are not limited by space or time, so walk freely around this Earth, and see that every corner is the manifestation of the Golden Age. It is already here and exists in the now. But you have to manifest this world in you first for it to be manifested physically. The world doesn't reach this point on its own. It gets there through you. You are what makes the world complete. Your projection of love makes it whole and love.

See this world, where we all live as One. As one heals, we all heal. As one loves, we all love. As one experiences joy, we all experience joy. So peace happens for us all, and it starts with you, with your vision and your desire to serve others. For you know, others are self, and self is others. And this desire comes from the deepest part of your heart and soul because the God Self in you recognises the God Self in all others, which can not leave anyone out.

So embrace the power you have as co-creator to create this Golden Age in God's image. As you see peace within you, you see Peace on Earth. You bring peace to the entire Universe.

From now on, you will stop looking for peace outside you. Instead, you will start looking for peace, the only place it can be found - in the kingdom of peace within you, in the Flame of Peace that I Am. You know the Elohim of Peace are willing to share with you as we dedicate yourself to peace regardless of external conditions.

And he says, "Thus, Peace be still and know that I AM God. Peace be still and know that I AM Presence within you is God. My peace I leave with you. Multiply it and radiate it to all life so that this planet can be a peace."

Beth Amine

Multi-media Artist. Dance Instructor.
Longevity Coach.

Beth Amine is a multi-media artist: author, painter, dancer, performer, speaker and teacher. She has dedicated the past 50 years to exploring well-being through artistic self-expression, celebration and engaging with community. Her passion is to encourage joyous everyday living for everyone. Working with thousands of individuals of every age, physical and mental ability, she has seen many miracles of released joy, physical and emotional stability and self-love where there was none before. *Joyous Every Day Living*, her first book, was published in 2017. It provides a system of interwoven qualities of aliveness that when embodied, create a life of perpetual joy, self-care and rejuvenation. Her current focus is *Dancing with Time*, programs for a new, fun, positive alternative to default aging.

www.BethAmine.com

Joyous Movement

IT IS OUR ESSENTIAL NATURE to flourish. Joy and well-being are our natural state and purpose, yet so many of us find it challenging to maintain or even reach this fundamental condition. Sharing excerpts from my book, *Joyous Every Day Living* which encourages you to consistently choose fresh and expansive possibilities for creating deep, personal joy. This overflowing enjoyment of life can then be shared with others.

Information that we constantly receive from a wide variety of external sources has a limiting message about our potential for living a long vibrant life. Our cultural paradigm insists that in life and the aging process, we must have an inevitable physical and mental decline. Yet we have the authority to consciously alter our expectations and generate our own positive outcomes. Often asking "What do I want?" and "What makes me feel good?" keeps us centered in answers that are the best choices for our individual lives.

Here is an excerpt from Chapter One of my book *Joyous Every Day Living*. It is entitled *Move* and is included here as an essential approach to life. More than moving just the body, it is the sense and practice of fluidity with all of life's shifting circumstances. It is truly Dancing with Time!

JOYOUS EVERY DAY LIVING BEGINS with a focus on movement, one of the basic qualifying components of being alive. The act of moving reflects our essential natures, which thrive in a constant state of expansion. Our purpose is to open and grow in sync with the Universe we live in, as we are eternal life forms moving through time. Physical movement is crucial to well-being on all levels of our experience.

It heals mind, body and emotions. Moving the body can be science, art, or even mystical experience. It is also the most primary way to create connection to self and the broader context of life. Dance movement, which unites our physical awareness with music, is the oldest known ritual for linking to forces greater than oneself. Since early human history, people have moved to the rhythm of their heart beat and simple percussion instruments to connect with and make sense of the vastness of experience.

Beyond its spiritual aspects, dance has been proven scientifically to be the number one activity for creating regeneration of brain cells and slowing the decline of mind and body. With consistent practice, agility, mobility and stability are sustained and the health of life-giving circulatory and respiratory systems can be maintained.

Simply put, dance is union. And most importantly, it is exhilarating fun!

I witness the miracles of movement constantly in my dance classes, which are for every level of fitness and cognitive ability. Individuals who did not smile, walk, or even lift their arms and breathe, come alive and vital when connecting their bodies to music. Others learn to shine and become unafraid to show up as who they essentially are. Dance movement has the power to create a deep healing bond between our internal life and basic sense of value or feelings of worthiness.

The theme of self-love is pervasive in this book as the essential component of both connection to feeling alive and to love and compassion for others. It is so beautiful and freeing to finally have the knowledge that we are worthy just because we are alive and therefore made of and from love. Creating a deep mind-body connection through music and movement roots this knowledge in our being.

There is a profound unifying beauty in feeling all aspects of life through the sensuality of our physical experience. The myth of scarcity and lack and therefore separation from the source of life goes very deep for us culturally.

The thoughts that there is not enough or I am not enough are omni-present.

One of the most challenging "not enoughs" for almost all of us is negative body judgment. Through movement, we join without thinking to our inner life and essential nature and can create complete freedom from this debilitating mind-set. Our thoughts create our reality. They can therefore create negative as well as positive conditions in our health and well-being. Dance is liberation into life-affirming choices.

Carole Fontaine

Inspirer. Adventurer. Lightworker.

Carole Fontaine is the author of *SAIL ABOVE THE CLOUDS—How to Simplify your Life*, a finalist in BOOK OF THE YEAR 2021 from Book Talk Radio Club, and bestseller on Amazon for weeks. Her memoir/self-improvement series sold across 5 continents and inspires hundreds with adventures, lessons, and self-mastery tools. Known to some as, "The Sailing Yogi," she studied holistic and yogic philosophies after her health failed and sent her on a decade-long search for answers on how to heal body and soul. She is passionate about helping others discover their mind/body/spirit connection and uses stories from her 20-years of living aboard a sailboat to inspire people to simplify their lives and find peace and purpose. Carole is a Mindfulness and Empowerment Guide, Meditative Writing, Shakti Dance® Yoga, and Reiki Master Teacher. She owns a thriving graphic design business and lives in Maine with her husband of 30 years.

www.SailAboveTheClouds.com

Blessed Are
The Tides of Life — Align With The Flow

"You are swimming in a sea of possibilities.
Don't fight the current."

The first rays of sunrise hit the water and instantly pierce through my sleeping eyelids. I open wide and look through the porthole barely eight inches from my nose, and see the most magnificent orange sliver calling me to rise. Hues of reds, oranges, and yellows cascade from the sun and radiate across the sea, kissing my face with the promise of a good day. I feel the warmth of my dog snuggled on top of the covers between me and my husband, hugging my back.

The only sound I can hear is their peaceful breathing, the gentle creaking of a boat at anchor, the occasional song from the wind whistling through the rigging, and the splattering of the water against the hull.

The sun, star of the show, performs its glowing entrance by reflecting across a sparkling blanket of water. I place my fingers on the hull of the boat where not even an inch separates me from endless miles of ocean and the sun, and imagine catching a ray in the palm of my hand. I make a mental note and commit to memory this feeling of absolute peace, of belonging and bearing witness to the beauty of life. This must be heaven. Safely tucked away aboard *Windsong*, a 41'

sailboat—our home for the last two decades—I revel in this new day.

I turn and look at the tanned, weathered face of my husband, tracing each wrinkle with my gaze. I know every minute detail of this face, a constant companion, cheering squad, trigger instigator, and best friend for the last 30 years. His blond hair is now white or as he likes to call it; platinum. We've traversed so many obstacles and traveled so far on our journey. It sometimes feels like we've spent many lifetimes together... and maybe we have.

We're on yet another adventure, exploring the East Coast and cruising north from Florida to Maine, approximately 1,200 nautical miles without counting my daily tourist detours and excursions. I'm nervous about moving back to northern climates after 25 years South but I've decided to give it a try and like every other time I've had to change my life, I have faith in what this new chapter will bring.

The hatch overhead floods the room with a warm morning glow and Dozer, aware of mommy's wakefulness, decides it's time for some tail-wagging and morning kisses. "Come on pumpkin, let's get up so we don't wake daddy!" I climb down and follow the dog into the galley. It's going to be warm today. Dozer asks for the "door" which on the boat means he stretches halfway up the ladder wanting out, so I bend down and give him a ride up and over the edge into the cockpit, an acrobatic trick we've perfected from

hundreds of climbs in the 5 years since we've adopted him. He's a happy boat dog.

I follow him on deck and stretch. The air is warm on my bare skin. I can smell the saltiness of the sea and the boat feels wet from the light dew. I love this time of day when the veil between night and day is just lifting and I still have one foot into the other realm. It's a time for introspection and meditation. The boat rises and falls with each wave as I balance myself on my yoga mat.

We are anchored at the entrance of a large bay with no one in sight. You could have drawn a picture of this beach 200 years ago and it would look the same, pristine scenery, the passage of time unmarked except for one small post on the deserted beach nearby, the only sign of human life.

Nature always reminds me of how vast the universe is and how infinitely small our problems are in the grand scheme of things. The cycle of life never stops, life goes on no matter what; birth, life, death, decay, rebirth. Constant transition and transformation. It puts things into perspective.

The morning tide will be taking over the beach soon, washing away the seashore then letting go and leaving behind a cleaned, polished beach. It's the original Etch-a-Sketch giving you an infinite amount of possibilities then erasing all creations, mistakes, masterpieces, and all. I appreciate the lesson. No

matter what you build or create in life — good or bad — it will eventually be washed away by the cycle of time and the only thing left will be your soul joining the stars.

There is much to be learned from Mother Ocean.

How many times have I lost sight of the shore — and myself — only to be reminded in the vastness of nothing that I am everything?

It's incredibly liberating and empowering to face your mortality aboard a small floating vessel in the middle of an oncoming storm. To realize that the purpose of life is to find yourself and the only way to do so is to let go of everything you thought you were supposed to be. How ironic!

I close my eyes and start to chant my morning mantras. Dozer likes to snuggle beside me on the mat and gives me wet kisses. I laugh at the tickles and scratch his head. "Good boy. I hear daddy stirring below. We'll go to the beach soon."

I feel blessed for having lived such a colorful life and having learned to follow the inner and outer currents calling me. It brought me here to this present day, alive and acutely aware of how precious every minute is. Braving hurricanes, raging seas and chronic illness have given me a deep sense of reverence for life and second chances.

I've developed an ability to adapt to change and tap into a source of strength and resilience I had no idea I possessed.

> I contemplate some of the cycles in my life…
> - from immigrating to the US and adapting to Florida life,
> - from trading my Harley Davidson leathers for flip-flops,
> - from working 9 to 5 to starting my own business,
> - from magazine publisher to bankruptcy,
> - from party girl to sailing yogi,
> - from landlubber to 20-years liveaboard sailor,
> - from wine abuser to Reiki master teacher
> - from graphic designer to crystal jewelry designer,
> - from snow to tropics to snow again,
> - from city life to island life,
> - from healthy beach body to chronic illness,
> - from depression to an empowered health advocate, lightworker, and mindfulness guide.

I've reinvented myself countless times, transitioning from one role to the next, evolving, growing, shedding skin, and discovering my resolve in answering the most profound question:

"Who am I?"

The answer stopped being an enigma the moment I changed my focus from the outside and dove within. In my darkest night of the soul, after years of misdiagnosis, surgeries, and failed treatments I cried out in pain and despair. A voice echoed back, "I am a soul. Death has no power over me. It is simply the beginning of another journey. If this is my time, so be it."

From this point forth, everything has been a bonus. A gift from the Goddess, a winning round that could have easily dissipated to dust. I promised myself that if I came out of this alive, I would not waste my time on mundane concerns and would live a purposeful life.

With a renewed sense of hope and a ferocious taste for living, I threw myself into yogic practices. I tapped into my Shakti energy with incredible courage and braved oncoming storms, learning to captain my 15-ton sailboat and navigate myself back to health. How far have I gone to find myself when I've been sitting here all along waiting?

I bring my attention back to the horizon where I sit witnessing the new day. I have learned to surrender everything to the cycles of times. Tides, currents, wave patterns, weather systems, all following their agenda, all I can do is stay true to myself, prioritize self-love, and navigate life with passion and purpose.

My quest lead me to four principles to SAIL the flow of life:

1. Simplify your life.
It will bring clarity and spiritual expansion.
2. Align yourself with joy.
It is where the divine flows and will guide you to purpose.
3. Integrate tools for success.
It will support your daily practice even on the worst days.
4. Let go of all that doesn't serve you.
It will free you to manifest your best and highest life.

Together, they helped me rise beyond the elements trying to rock my world and S.A.I.L. above the clouds. Experiences shape us but do not define us. Living with physical or mental health issues is challenging. Because I needed to rise above the drama and trauma that caused me pain I created a treasure map that shows me the way. S.A.I.L.™ (Simplify, Align, Integrate, Let go) is my lighthouse in the middle of a storm.

I rise saluting the sun as Eric pops his head out of the companionway and says, "Ready?" Dozer runs to the back of the boat, knowing it's time to go to the beach. We hop in the tender and cover the short distance as Dozer tries to bite oncoming waves. He looks at us dripping wet and grinning, and we laugh at his playfulness. As soon as we are within feet of the beach, he jumps in, unable to contain his excitement. The tide has taken over almost every grain of sand but that doesn't curb his enthusiasm as he runs free, eager

to explore all that it has to offer. There is a lesson here.

Open yourself to a world of possibilities no matter how meek the circumstances may be. There are opportunities hidden in every situation if you allow your heart to guide you. And just like the ocean releases a polished and glistening beach, I let go of my fears and trust in the returning tides. Today is a good day for new adventures. I will raise my sails and follow my North Star.

Om Shanti.

Cheryl Partridge

Global Spiritual Teacher. Homeschool Mom.
Healer. Homesteader.

Cheryl Partridge is from a small village in the heart of Maine. She is a partner of *Wild Ones Academy Homeschool and Homestead* and troop leader for "Rainbow Rangers." She is a homesteader and healer, whose spiritual calling and abilities manifested by the age of nine years old. After 27 years in the wellness industry and a career opening, owning and operating spas, she was struck with a debilitating illness that left her bedridden off and on for years. She dove deep into her relationship with the Sacred Divine, opening up fully to what has become her life's work, *"The Sacred Women Principles."* These principles healed Cheryl and are the foundation for which she uses to guide and support each person to that place of true change and healing.

www.SacredSisterhoodTribe.com

Sacred
Women Principles
(An introduction)

In The Beginning:

Being a woman in this world is such an incredibly powerful time right now. Our wombs the connection from this earth to the heavens. Remembering who we are as women is vital for our humanity. Understanding our Twelve Principles will create real change within not just you but this world. To do this we all have to come together remembering who we are as women. Understanding we are all on the same journey even if it looks much different then our own. We understand that if we truly want to heal and change this world we have to do this work in our own home.

Practicing these Twelve Sacred Women Principles simultaneously honoring our sacred Four Season cycle of menstruation will create the LIFE you have always wanted for yourself. You will see the world shift in a multitude of miracles around you. You will become what you intend to be. You are that powerful!

Our first step into awakening to who we really are is remembering we ARE the ultimate superpower in our lives. We do have the power to change this world but we collectively need your full participation. This happens when we take responsibility for our own self.

Each principle guides us closer to evolving and changing. With that change a new life emerges. We are the shift and we are the change as long as we are able to take back control of our own lives and remember who we are. By shifting ourselves to a higher state of consciousness we then are able to have influence for others to do the same.

My Personal Story

How did I come upon these Sacred Women Principles? I hear stories like this one from others but I never thought I would be here telling you my story. The fact that I have lived this story still amazes me. The amount of bravery I needed to step into to bring you these principles has been more than I would have realized. Although the pull has been so strong I could no longer deny it. The creator has been speaking to me for as long as I can remember. I had been a study of these principles unbeknownst to me since I was a little girl.

These principles came to me in pieces starting at age nine years old. I was the naughty child who questioned everything. I NEW a teaching was not from God and would passionately challenged my Sunday school teacher. I was taken one day to father Bob to have a swift talking to about my behavior. He looked at me with the most kindest grin you could imagine. He told me how proud he was of me. He talked to me about Jesus and his own journey. How I have now

come to place of what it means to truly listen within. To study all faiths, beliefs and experiences. After a great big hug I walked out of his office and into the truth I am teaching you today.

My story became an adventure like your would see in a story book. I studied many faiths. I had many traumas and uncomfortable experiences. I also had many glorious journeys and miracles all throughout my life.

After my second relapse of my chronic condition (doctors still do not know what I have) God/Source came to me while breastfeeding Sophia. It's an incredible story that one day I will bore you with but for now our focus is you.

They told me to put together what I now know is our

12 Principles Of Life. I have always known these Principles but until that day I did not know how to put them together for others to experience. These principles are focused on women but these principles can also be practiced by our incredible and amazing men. I would like to add before we walk this journey of remembering who we are as women is to take a special pause to honor our sacred men. To walk our journey as women we need to remember we are not men and that is such a beautiful thing. Men hold a sacred space in our life even if we do not feel a romantic connection to them. They provide for us something women are not supposed to hold. Which is why we give them so much thanks and gratitude for being who they are.

For the men we do relate these principles to our unique superpower which is our four seasons of menstruation. You also have this super power within you but it looks much different than women. We need you to BE YOU exactly who you are so that we may experience all pieces and sides of ourselves.

Each principle will bring you to an awareness of who you are and where you want to go. Moving you forward into forever evolving into the best versions of yourself. As we evolve we impact not just ourselves but our relationships and the world. We do this by focusing on one Principle per. month each week walking along our life map and following our inner compass.

We come to an awareness we are self but we are also part of a much larger whole. When we solely focus on the self but many pieces of self to create a whole self. Our relationships help support our developments and awareness of who we are. Even the relationships which only last for a few moments or ones that make us feel uncomfortable. From those relationships we impact 80,000 people in our lifetime. Each of those lives you have touched impacts their own 80,000 people. The ripple effect of your interactions affects the whole world. Yes , YOU and just you have an enormous impact with every single person you are in contact with. We can change this world but it has to start with us AT HOME. How you walk along your map of life. How you live your life. How you love yourself. How you treat others. Every single thing

you do is so incredibly powerful. You and only you have this unique mark in the world that only you can give. Without you this world would never be the same. Thank you from the bottom of my heart that you are in this world with me. I have always needed you. Knowing how many people you have touched I know that at some point I have been touched by your impact. I in turn do the same for you.

I hope your journey with me finds you PEACE, LOVE and HAPPINESS!!! I am not walking in front of you or behind you. I am walking hand in hand with you. I am on the same journey as you are. I will forever be learning, evolving, and walking towards the best versions of myself. I am grateful to have you walk beside me. With love, support and compassion we can live a life of PEACE, JOY, and HAPPINESS.

Your Spirit Sister.

On the following pages Cheryl has shared
a sample ceremony:
"Sacred Sisterhood Circle of Healing"
as well as a *"Prayer For Healing."*

"Sacred Sisterhood Circle Of Healing"

Purpose of Ceremony:

Creating a place where women can support one another and be supported themselves. To have the opportunity to remember who they truly are and to give them the tools they need to courageously step out as their authentic selves. Celebrating together a sense of sisterhood with other women during the power cycles of the four seasons of women's menstrual cycle. This ceremony will bring wombs and hearts to a place of healing and letting go so women can move into their true intentions of what they are meant to do here on earth. Designed with the understanding that each of us are incredibly important and we need to be heard, supported and loved in a way that brings us a sense of peace, ease, joy and kindness.

Sacred Ceremony

What you will need:
- your Sacred Circle of women;
- candles (1 dark candle, 1 white candle);
- community alter;
- blankets, pillows;
- oracle cards;
- healing instruments (drums, crystals etc.);
- healing music;
- and chocolate *(the best part!)*.

Step 1

Opening Circle Prayer

We are here to celebrate our connection to each other, to recognize our accomplishments, to welcome our awareness. We are here to bless our paths in life, our chance to grow and learn, our sacred cycles, our loved ones, our health, our creations, our home, where we live, what we have, and who we are.

We ask our highest source of Divine of Love, Peace, Kindness and Compassion and to all of our highest helpers to awaken our true self with no apology. To help us remember who we are, where we have come from and help gently and with ease in the direction of our own journey.

As women we gather in a form of a circle shoulder to shoulder, facing center, witness and witnessing, creating a sisterhood of empowering each other unconditionally. As women in our sacred 28-day cycle of power we become aware of the magic that is us. As women we are messy, we are connected, we are intuitive, we are wise, and we are wild and free.

The four seasons happen in nature and all around us. But it also happens inside of us, in our souls. It can happen inside of us in summer or winter, spring or fall. In the still place of our soul, we carry secret wishes, pains, frustrations, loneliness, fears, regrets, and worries.

Becoming awake as we pass through from one season to the next season is not something to be afraid of. Sometimes we go to the still place of our soul, where we can find safety and comfort. Becoming awake and needing to move can be happy and joyous but growing pains can also be painful. Moving forward can awaken what no longer serves us. This could mean people, places and comforts that need to be shed to allow our spirit to move forward in growth and the direction that our soul is asking to move. As we let go of the old we now make room for the new.

Step 2
I now ask for all of us to hold hands.
Feel the circle of women who are here to support you and hold on to you in your spring growth.
3 Cleansing breaths
It is now time to LET GO
What were you made aware of in this season of your life?

Feel the energy of your sisters around you. Feel the support we are giving you right now. We are not here to give advice or to help you fix. Understanding as women we have an intense desire to do so. In this moment on this day it is about witnessing and supporting one another as we are in our journey.
3 Cleansing breaths again

Oracle Cards Can Be Used Here
Now we will pick a card that will guide us in our journey of growth. We ask our highest Devine and all of our highest to give us a message that we may understand.

Now that we have picked a card: Let us share just a few sentences of how this card is true for you and maybe it is not true for you. I ask everyone to please be a whiteness and an observer for our sister's growth and not try to offer advice or a relatable story that may impact our sisters own journey.

Step 3
Sacred Women's Circle

Three Parts Of Our Circle:

Source- She is the most important woman of this circle. She will be letting go of all that does not serve her. She will have the opportunity to heal and give birth as she reenters into her new world of possibilities.

· She is the center of the circle.

· She is to feel her body, emotions and spirit.

· She is to release all that no longer serves her.

· She will allow midwives and warriors to protect and support her.

· She will ask for help when needed.

· When finished she will rise and gather her candle that has been placed below her feet.

· At the ceremonial bowl she will light the candle and burn all that does not serve her.

Midwives- Women, you are the healers, the wise woman, deer goddess and crows of the sources circle. Allow your spirit and emotions to guide your hands and voice

in connecting with the source. Trust your own inner goddess to what her "source" needs.
· Use safe touch.
· Be the conduit of energy from the highest and loving source.
· Support "source" with anything she may need while birthing.

Warriors- You are the protectors of energy and love. Your job is to keep the circle pure and of love. Any observation that does not serve the circle in their highest it is your job to clear it.
· Observe any discomfort. Use your inner woman wisdom and when being called use sage, bells, rattles or drums to clear the area.
· Gather a glass of water, tissues or anything might be needed while circle is in progress. When the "source" has finished guide her to the lighting ceremony.

Time For Healing
It is now time for the healing to begin.
Please have blankets ready.
Have your music on.
Your candles in position and you may begin.

1. Choose who your "source" will be and allow her to lay comfortably on the ground or on a massage table. Blankets and coverings are encouraged.

2. Allow "Source" to pick her midwives. Everyone's participation is vital for healing but midwives are very personal.

3. Warriors, you are her protector. Please surround the "source" and midwives.

Now that everyone is in place you may begin the ceremony of healing. Each woman has a turn being source, midwife and warrior. Once everyone has been through the "Letting Go" ceremony it is now time to bring your "Seeds Of Intentions."

Planting Your Seeds Of Intentions

Prayer

~We call upon the Earth, our planet home, with its beautiful depths and soaring heights, its vitality and abundance of life...

~We call upon the mountains...the high green valleys and meadows filled with wildflowers, the snows that never melt, the summits of intense silence...

~We call upon the waters that rim the earth, horizon to horizon, that flow in our rivers and streams, that fall upon our gardens and fields...

~We call upon the forests, the great trees reaching strongly to the sky with earth in their roots and the heavens in their branches, the fir, pine and cedar...

~We call upon the creatures of the fields and forests and the seas, our sisters the wolves and deer, the eagle and dove, the great whales and dolphins, the beautiful Orca and the salmon...

~We call upon all those who have lived on this earth, our ancestors and our friends, who dreamed the best for future generations, and upon whose lives our lives are built...

~And lastly, we call upon all that we hold most sacred, the presence and power of the Great Spirit of love and truth which flows through all the universe, to be with us to Teach us, and show us the way.

Reflection Circle Of Intentions

It is now time to sit back in a circle shoulder to shoulder. Please place a white candle in front of you. One at a time answer these questions.

· What will be your seed that you now have room to plant? I recommend using one or two words that symbolize your intentions such as trust, feeling present, abundant etc.

· Light your candle and say your intention 3 times while holding your candle.

· It is now time to place your intentions on the community table with all the other intentions.

· A bowl of purifying water will be provided for purity for washing your hands.

· A midwife will then towel off and dry hands and provide you with chocolate.

I recommend no talking to make sure each woman may complete her sacred ceremony.

The ceremony has now been completed. You will feel the healing powers and enjoy.

Prayer For Healing

Source of Divine love and the healing power
of grace, peace, kindness and communication.

I place your gentle care our need for healing.
And the healing power for my friends, family,
neighbors and especially my enemies.

I now ask you to fill our hearts with your
transcending and transforming love.

I now ask you to heal our life that we may receive
your unconditional love and healing.

We ask for healing especially for…
(to yourself or out loud name person(s))

(Moment of silence)

As we accept and receive this amazing blessing
all wounds and pain offered up to you.

Danielle Dufour

Spiritual Mentor. Empath. Medium.

Rev. Danielle Dufour, B.Msc, DPSW, has worked directly in the Human Services Field(s) since she was 18 years old. She offers her gifts helping people discover, process, and release emotional and/or physical pain from their bodies. Danielle is able to channel information from divine source in a variety of ways, and facilitate the experience a person or group most needs to optimally feel deep inner connections and energetic shifts for themselves. She is passionate about teaching people how to see, feel, and practice healing through the Human Energy Field. Danielle is certified as a Quantum Touch Energy Practitioner, a Yoga Teacher, and an Integrative Counselor. She is an Ordained Minister and Wedding Officiant, as well as a Lake and Moving Water Canoe Instructor.

"I love facilitating and supporting a person during and after they have experienced a profound healing, affirming moment, or anything in between."

www.LifeForceEnergy.net

Mystical Messages

I have been channeling what I'm calling Mystical Messages lately. When I channel these messages, I just ask a question and then the answer I receive is very quick. I have included three Mystical Messages that stand out for me right now and what we are all experiencing...globally.

Mystical Message: How can I keep my faith during unsettling times?

To be real with yourself and develop understanding is key; first creating self understanding and then self-healing and growth. There will never be a perfect time for your ego mind, but there is perfection in every moment for your high mind; for your God mind.

Not being fearful to pray to God, fearful that your prayers won't be heard. When praying from a place of deep inner confidence, there is no need to beg and plea for this or that, but to know deeply that all will be given to you as your life purpose unfolds. Trusting that when you receive inner guidance, inspiration, or a creative notion, that it comes from a higher place, therefore, a knowingness and confidence must exude that God, Universe, Higher Self, or with whom or what you most resonate with, will and has already provided you with all that you need to be successful. Roads wander here and there. Travel as the wind blows, follow your heart wisdom, ask questions of your higher self and listen as the answers come in intricate unexpected ways.

Your human vessel is one of strength and durability. Remembering the limitless mechanics of what you are. "The value of life lies not in the length of days, but in the use we make of them".

Mystical Message: How can humans become more intuitive?

Daily application is key. Diving into the wonders of everything that exists and how it is interconnected, going beyond what one can see in everyday life.

If that's the case, then what is there to rely ones perceptions upon? Everything humans absorb in their atmosphere is reflected within them. It is when knowingness is allowed to take hold that this is realized.

There is no right or wrong way to remember ones souls abilities. The zest for life is what will draw one closer to oneself. Closer to source, creator, God, the universe; all what one perceives and has resonance with.

Take heed in what is before you in each situation. Be willing to become quiet in any form and when thoughts come in, where are they coming from? Pay attention. And follow up with action.

Taking great energy in noticing your energy; your vibration, and your frequency. As this is what you are projecting like a boomerang it will return. When light and love exude, then this is returned ten fold.

The butterfly effect is real like dominos on a beautiful shimmering golden board, or a match of light that ignites an entire world. Your light is the way, seeing your bright light and remembering your truth. Carry on with courage as your beautiful journey awaits.

Mystical Message: How do I stay positive around dense or low vibrational energy?

Thoughts are the most important thing. Remind yourself to have a conversation with yourself and not feel foolish or silent. There are many things we can learn about ourselves if we allow ourselves to look, to see, to feel. If vibrational energy is low look inside you, and see what you can do about that.

Rise up to meet your soul's true energetic frequency of light and love. No this is not silly or misguided, this is powerful and true. Allow the strong winds to flood your soul with passionate desire. It is only when we snuff out light and fall to earthly illusion that we lose our place and begin to feel dense.

Denseness is a state of mind, being, and soul. We are here on this plane to evolve, learn , grow, and have fun with our characters. Be grande in them, see yourself rising above the clouded illusion that has masked our plane for indescribable time. Stay only focused on what you hear and see inside you.

Ask yourself, who is talking when you hear or feel strong intuition? Is it you? Or something grander, connecting you, reminding you, that you are one with the beautiful artistry of the divine. The moment you allow yourself to remember this, the sooner you will rise to such a high vibration that you will only lift others and proudly just be your best human self.

Deana Sanderson

Energy Specialist. Yoga Instructor. Aromatherapist.

Rev. Deana Sanderson, B.Msc., MBA, RYT-200, HTP, CAHP is an Ordained Metaphysical Minister, Energy Specialist, and Self-Care Wellness Coach. Utilizing spiritual practices, Deana teaches others how to heal the conditions of their physical, emotional, mental, and spiritual bodies. She specializes in biofield healing therapy and helps individuals navigate their current belief system to uncover patterns, ways of being, that contribute to their physical and mental dis-ease. Deana is also a registered yoga teacher who designs programs to help people develop a greater sense of presence and self-awareness. In addition to inspiring others and teaching how to live from a place of love, acceptance, and compassion, Deana is a certified aromatherapist. She formulates and manufactures natural plant-based skincare products as well creates synergistic treatment blends using essential oils to target specific clinical symptoms and restore emotional and spiritual balance.

www.DeanaSanderson.com

Journey Through
the Chakras

For a lot of people, their physical reality is all that exists. Anything outside of what can be perceived using the five senses (sight, touch, taste, smell, and sound) doesn't hold truth. The fact of the matter is ALL physical matter IS energy. This is true for our physical bodies and the organs within, chemical compounds naturally found in nature, the food we consume, our loving pets that share our lives, the furniture we sit on, everything is energy including inanimate objects. There is more to you than just your physical body! You exist inside your physical being as well outside your physical structure. You are pure energy! Some of that energy manifests as your physical body, and some manifests as your human energy field (auric field). Every part of you, physical or auric, is made up of oscillating strands of energy.

We are all varying manifestations of the one true source. The human body we inhabit is designed with specific energy systems that connect our physical body to our auric field. It is within these energy systems we can create balance and harmony to bring about healing. Working with the auric body, also known as the biofield, we can bring overactive (excess) energy states in balance, underactive (deficient) energy states in balance as well remove any blocked, stagnant energy. Our aura is an electromagnetic

shield that surrounds the physical body and expands approximately 3 feet, in all directions. It is an electro-dynamic protective shield that guides us as we make our journey through life. This subtle energy field can also inform and reveal future states. Abnormalities present in the auric body long before they manifest as illness or disease in the human body. These deviations, energy inconsistencies, can be detected in a person's aura when receiving biofield healing therapy. A rebalancing of energies can help ward off mental disparities such as anxiety and depression as well help prevent physical disease resulting from immune and/ or autonomic nervous system disorders. An optimally functioning and balanced auric field is necessary in maintaining health. When our energy flows freely, unhindered, in a balanced fashion, the result is health, happiness, and harmony.

The auric body is formed by the energy centers that interpenetrate with our human structure. Also know as chakras, these subtle energy centers allow us, as physical Beings, to communicate with our external environment. Our chakras also enable our external world to communicate with our internal Self. These specialized energy collection and transmission centers are divinely designed to shift energy from a higher to a lower vibration as well from lower to higher vibration.

There are many chakras in and around our physical body. We have secondary chakras dispersed throughout our body including the tips of our fingers, palms and soles of our hands and feet, in every joint,

and on every organ. We have seven primary chakras that exist along the main branching's of our nervous system and are each associated with an endocrine gland. The major chakras include the root, sacral, solar plexus, heart, throat, brow, and crown. Think of these energy centers as your operating system with each chakra coded with a specific program.

The root chakra is aligned on the coccygeal nerve plexus and is associated with the adrenal glands. This energy center contains your survival program. If your first energy center is functioning harmoniously you will find it easy to achieve goals. You perceive the earth as a secure and safe place in which all your needs are met. You trust yourself as well others and express gratitude in your life. If, on the other hand, your root chakra is congested you may experience thoughts and/or actions that primarily revolve around material possessions and indulgences. You may find it difficult to meet the demands of life and have feelings of uncertainty and worry. Life may seem like a burden instead of a pleasure and you may long for an easier, less strenuous, way of life.

The second energy center, the sacral chakra, is your sexual program and center for emotions. This chakra is located on the sacral nerve plexus and is associated with the gonads (testes in males, ovaries in females). When your sacral energy center is functioning harmoniously you participate in the deep joy of creation and life with enthusiasm and awe. You feel the flow of creative life energy streaming

through your Spirit, Mind, and Body. You enjoy a healthy relationship with yourself as well others. An unbalanced sacral center can often be traced back to early childhood experiences. Lack of affection, tenderness, and gentle touches from caregivers results in a malfunctioning sacral chakra. Suppressed feelings and withdrawal from yourself and others also present when the second center is not functioning in a harmonious manner. Sexually, a deficient sacral center manifests diminished, repressed or nonexistent sexual feelings. This may lead to negation and rejection of sexuality in later years.

The solar plexus contains your personal power and self-esteem program code. The third energy center is located on the solar plexus nerve plexus and associates with the pancreas endocrine gland. It is within this chakra you will experience a feeling of inner peace and harmony if it is in a balanced state. When the third center is functioning harmoniously, you accept yourself completely as well respect the feelings and character traits of others. When your solar plexus center is not healthy, you are easily upset and agitated. You feel the need to manipulate your surroundings according to your own wishes. You want to control, have power over, both your inner and outer world.

The next chakra, the heart center, contains the code for your relationship program. The fourth chakra is located on the cardiac plexus and relates to the thymus gland. This energy center is the bridge

that connects the physical characteristics of our being with the higher, spiritual aspects. This gateway between the spiritual and material world is associated with our relationships and how we interact with other people, animals, plants, inanimate objects, the earth, the universe, as well the relationship we have with ourselves. If your fourth center is balanced and functioning harmoniously, you love and accept yourself as well honor your individuality and that of others. You have strong relationships with family and friends. If your heart chakra is not functioning optimally, you may find it difficult to empathize and sympathize with others. You struggle with self-acceptance and self-love as well feel overwhelmed by others.

The fifth center, throat chakra, is known as your language program. This energy center is located on the cervical ganglia medulla nerve plexus and connects with the thyroid gland. A balanced throat center communicates the truth of one's experience. You feel connected and maintain order in your life. You have good communication skills, are an effective listener, and not bound by fear to accept certain ways of doing things. If, on the other hand, your fifth center is in an unbalanced state you will not be orderly in your life or feel connected to your surroundings. You will find it difficult to speak your truth and may find it difficult to understand complicated systems or patterns.

The brow chakra, also known as the third eye, is our visual and intuitive program. It is located on the carotid nerve plexus and associates with the pineal

endocrine gland. A balanced brow center has the characteristics of intuitive perceptive abilities that enhance one's functioning and ability to be creative and imaginative. When your sixth center is not balanced, you lack spiritual nourishment and cannot imagine different or varying outcomes. You are unable to find a guiding vision that gives meaning to life.

The crown center contains our belief system program and is located on the cerebral cortex nerve plexus associating with the pituitary gland. A balanced crown chakra enables creativity and the ability to clearly understand broad overall concepts about existence. You know where you fit in and have a strong spiritual connection. If the seventh chakra is in an unbalanced state, you are not able to accept imperfections in yourself or others.

There are many reasons why your energy system may be blocked or in an unbalanced state. Illness, injury, negative thoughts, misunderstandings, relationship issues, poor nutrition, lack of movement, emotional pain, spiritual concerns, and childhood issues or traumas are all examples of how your energy system can become overactive, underactive, and/or blocked.

From a physical perspective, if you suffer from chronic back pain, sciatica, varicose veins, depression, or immune-related disorders you could have a congested root chakra.

If you have obstetrical/gynecology problems, suffer from pelvic and/or low back pain, experience urinary tract issues, or have addictions, you may have an unbalanced sacral center.

Congested solar plexus chakras are associated with physical dysfunctions that include arthritis, gastric or duodenal ulcers, colon/intestinal issues, pancreatitis, diabetes, indigestion, chronic or acute anorexia or bulimia, liver dysfunction, and/or hepatitis.

Physical presentations such as asthma, allergies, lung cancer, bronchial pneumonia, upper back and shoulder area soreness or stiffness is associated with the heart center.

If your throat center is in an unbalanced state, you could experience a raspy throat, chronic sore throat, mouth ulcers, gum difficulties, temporomandibular joint problems (TMJ), scoliosis, laryngitis, swollen glands, or encounter thyroid problems.

Frequent headaches, nightmares, eyestrain, and blurred vision may indicate a congested brow center while the feeling of alienation, confusion, boredom, apathy, and the inability to learn may indicate an unbalanced crown chakra.

It's important to note here that while biofield healing therapy is an important and beneficial protocol to use when treating energy centers that are not in a balanced state, it does not replace allopathic treatment.

Energy therapy is not a standalone, replacement or alternative to medical treatment. Energy therapy compliments allopathic medicine.

Using techniques such as energy therapy, meditation, affirmations, breathing, physical exercise and visualizations, we can influence our chakras, our health, and our lives.

Step into the light and align with your greater purpose, your reason for being, your truth.

Believe and have faith in your True Self, your inner light, to guide and direct you as you journey through life.

Erin Colene

Life-style Coach. Writer. Self-Love Enthusiast.

Erin Colene is a healthy lifestyle coach, writer, day dreamer, and self-love enthusiast. She is a passionate advocate about healthy living. She inspires women to design a life that they really, truly love. She teaches that there are five main elements of health: *emotional, spiritual, physical, mental, & financial*. And that it's important that each of these categories get the love and attention they deserve! She loves to help women to align their head with their heart and their guts to eliminate *the shoulds* and the *I don't knows* & the *I'm sorrys* and move mindfully into inspired & empowered action. From this place, women are better able to create a life they feel good about. She assures we can reach a harmonious flow when we embrace what we value and most desire.

www.ErinColene.com

Lighter
(Let it Go!)

"Human warmth and openness will always be our only place of true safety. Be careful about hiding yourself away, because walls that are meant to be fortresses can quickly turn into prisons."
-Unknown (to me, anyways)

I came across this quote I had written on a piece of paper- who knows how long ago! It stopped me right in my tracks. I cried. I've never been a person with very good boundaries when it comes to other people because I just love people so much! I've had to practice this skill of having boundaries in every area of my life. I've been practicing for years, learning more and more about boundaries and their importance every day!

I realized the other day is that boundaries go both ways- around what we are letting in, and what we are giving out. Boundaries is also about leaning on our trusted people when we need to & accepting the love and support from our pillars of strength- whatever or whomever they may be. Boundaries are about giving and receiving.

So here we are, the seasons are changing (it's Autumn-time as I write), and I find myself digging deeper, only to let go deeper, and fill my cup up with Truth and with Love instead of fear and doubt.

I also love the quote, *"Autumn shows us how beautiful it is to let things go."* The trees teaching us about letting go.

"Let it go" has been the slogan, it seems, for the last few years. It feels like everywhere I look is another "let it go" cup or sweatshirt or song or whatever- it's so trendy! But actually- it's really freaking hard to do (for me, anyhow)! And my first thought is to let go of certain people that bring me down, then I think of decluttering my house... but what I'm learning is that maybe - it starts in our minds and our beliefs.

When we are younger, we learn tools to cope with situations that happen. But as we grow older, we have a greater capacity to handle certain situations and we also learn new tools to help us cope. So it becomes very important that we realize which beliefs and patterns of behaviors we are carrying with us, and which ones we can let go of so that we can use the new tools we have acquired. We learn more about our boundaries and creating healthier ones.

Recently, I have been focused on putting down the weight of other people's expectations of me. I've also been mindful to put down self-criticism and over functioning to prove my value/worth. I didn't even know I was doing this - until fairly recently. But simply watching myself react and then training myself to respond more mindfully has been a real game-changer! It's not easy work, my friends - and it's not particularly pretty either! But it's so worth it.

Another weight I've been carrying is thinking that I needed to do it all alone - so that no one else had to 'carry' my burdens with me. Becoming aware of this way of thinking/behaving has shifted everything in my closest relationships. After all, the foundation of healthy relationships is that people can show up authentically and be loved completely for exactly who they are- have support when they need it and lend support when needed.

So friends, what are you carrying? What can you (like the leaves) let go of this season? What support systems do you have in place? I'd love to hear!

Sending BIG hugs and love! I hope you feel all wrapped up in the coziest of blankets and held so tenderly!

The above is an excerpt originally posted on Erin's Blog. Be sure to take time to comment: https://erincolene.com/lighter/

Fatima Al-Sayed

Truth-Seeker. Intuitive. Free.

Fatima Al-Sayed, Ph.D. is a doctor of philosophy, specializing in holistic life counseling, a Reiki master and an EFT practitioner. Fatima uses her gifts to help bring clarity to herself and her clients. She is highly intuitive, and being a migraine and chronic headache sufferer herself for many years, she understands pain. Fatima looks at life from a holistic approach, so it comes naturally to her to lead others in putting their fingers on the aspects of their pain. Her diverse background enables her to connect with people from all walks of life. Her high regard to her clients' confidentiality, the absolute absence of judgment and the respect she shows to their journey, create a safe space for them to open up and explore the core of their suffering. She is spiritual, and believes that there is nothing that cannot be healed when we are connected to our Source of existence; The One Universal Truth.

www.holistic-life-counseling.webnode.com

Healing Journey

Who amongst us doesn't aspire to be healed physically, emotionally or spiritually? Who amongst us is above the need to be healed or has been immune to being hurt, wounded, wronged or struck by some sort or level of an ailment throughout their life journey? Who doesn't have hopes of a better life, a better health or a happier heart? If we take a moment to reflect, we won't need long to realize that humanity, and the planet we live on, is in desperate need of healing. Our present as well as our past need healing in order for us to move forward to a better existence. Our social structures are hurting, hospital beds are almost always fully booked, doctors are overworked and environmentalist are not winning their rightfully protested arguments.

This is not a pessimistic outlook at life but rather a statement that reflects a side of reality that we wish was a little rosier.

While giant industries have evolved on the very basis of the need to heal and many commercial, educational and many other private sectors have thrived on those needs, an important question remains open, are we there yet? Have we as individuals healed? Have we as communities healed? Have we as nations healed? The constant flow of news on conflicts, whether political around the world, or personal in our close surroundings, and the emerging new dis-

eases do not indicate that. So, what went wrong? What is it that we are not doing right in order to fix what is wrong with us? Do we need to address our issues on a national scale, a smaller scale or on a very individualistic basis?

In his book *A New Earth,* Eckhart Tolle addresses the readiness of humanity for a transformation of consciousness. Unless we evolve spiritually and awaken enough to take accountability and necessary actions towards our suffering, we will continue to hurt, some of us in silence. The human suffering will continue to be fed by the on-going wars against diseases, drugs, crimes and the list goes on. "Are we ready for such a transformation?" (Tolle, Eckhart. A New Earth; Awakening to your Life's Purpose. Plume, Penguin Group. USA. 2006.)

Pain and suffering are synonymous to living. Yet, they do not have to prevail in anyone's life but they are bound to manifest in one form or another at varying scales. The pursuit to eliminate pain, emotional or physical, and achieve wellness, which is our birth right, is a path we all go through at different stages of our physical existence. And whether we are aware of it or not, we play a significant role in creating our reality of illness or wellness. Striving for a better existence, we all must go through healing, and before exploring the concept of healing, we must explore the factors of our sickness first, the Body-Mind-Spirit relationship and how that relationship contributes to our well or ill-being.

Healing may take many shapes. For some of us, it may appear to be needed on the physical aspect. For others the need to heal may appear to be emotional or spiritual. In fact, we cannot settle for choosing one or the other, as healing is an integrated process that we have no control over, favoring one shape over another in order to suit our own perception of our needs.

My personal healing journey has led me to avenues that opened up a world of opportunities for me. I experienced successes and set-backs. I was led to learn new skills only to find that healing, while attainable, is not just a destination that we should seek, but it is a path to be walked if we wanted to have a healthy life journey. Life, simply, continues to happen. We go through changes, we have breakups, we experience losses. Events outside our control and other people's behaviors and decisions affect us and will have an impact on us. But we can shape this impact if we are healed and prepared to act from a neutral healthy space which can only happen while we are on the healing quest.

The need to heal is a given, but as life keeps happening, it is not enough to heal and expect to sit still and live happily ever after. It is rather a continuous journey, it is almost a daily endeavor for the pursuit of a better life, better health and ultimately a better "New Earth."

Healing is possible, when we are open to embrace a new way of thinking, a new style of living and a whole new level of understanding of who we are.

My own, once chronic, headache taught me how to live in the light of awareness. Awareness of the thought process, of the beliefs behind the thoughts, my response to the outer world, the connection to inner world and most importantly that with the Higher Power I believe in.

It is my finding through this journey that to live well is a product of elevated awareness and a collection of conscious choices we constantly have to make. The rest is just knowledge that we collect and apply along the way.

A healthy life is that of a continuous growth. Growth at the cellular level, as well as that of the soul. However, it is inhibited by toxicity. Toxicity is harmful to our bodies, our minds and to our hearts as well. Therefore, it is our biggest responsibility towards ourselves to maintain clean inner and outer worlds.

Our inner mental world can be kept clean by understanding our own thought patterns, maintaining positive attitudes and keeping contact with the Source of All That Is. Our hearts can be kept clean, by letting go of old hurts, practicing forgiveness and kindness to all and tapping into the love that is almost as essential for us humans, as the air we breathe. Our outer world can be maintained by balanced diet, clean physical environment, appropriate boundaries and healthy relationships.

To care for these two worlds properly, the

learnings need to be applied daily. The right choices need to be made constantly and the mental attitude need to be under continual monitoring. It is essential that we apply mindfulness and have gratitude in our daily lives. It is also essential that we live in the present and let go of all distractions and attachments that may pull us elsewhere.

Connecting to our Higher Power daily through prayers, meditation and giving up the need to be right will dim the ego self, avoiding conflicts and allowing kindness instead. Dealing with our issues and creating the appropriate mental environment will then make healing possible.

Living by those values throughout will keep us balanced and make it difficult for dis-ease to manifest.

It does not matter what we believe in, our backgrounds, our stories or the choices we make when we decide to take a healing journey, be it through spiritual growth, elimination of physical or emotional pain or a pursue of an improvement of life conditions. What matters is the need to keep moving forward on the chosen path. We cannot afford to sit still because it is not possible to go through life unaffected by the countless, complex dynamics of emotional plays involved. Hence it is necessary to put into daily practice, the learnings we are gathering from the valuable lessons the Universe puts in our way. It is a journey for life indeed.

Jaishree Dow-Spielman

Ascension Coach. Author. Singer. Musician.

Jaishree Deborah Dow-Spielman is an Ascension Coach, Author, and a life-long Singer/Musician. She is the Creator of Soul Mapping Matrix, a digital course on creating sacred space and staying sovereign, as well as Founder and Lead Educator of the Soul Culture Yoga School. Her mission is to share ancient wisdom, hold space and engage her clients in a co-creative process of experiencing the light of their own Truth go on. She calls this 1:1 coaching method Soul Mapping. She views her role in life is to mirror and elevate the highest essential beingness of every single person she meets. She has degrees in theatre, religion and ethics, master certifications in the yogas and various energy healing modalities, and countless hours at the feet of wisdom keepers and lineage holders. She has helped thousands of people seeking the light of their own truth and empowerment to create their own Soul Culture.

www.JaishreeYoga.com

Soul Ascension:

SURRENDER

Ascension means flowing with reality, holding the intensity, the possibility, and the unknown while moving forward with it. This world is being presented with unprecedented change. It is not slowing down, it is accelerating. Technology, media, politics, health care, freedom, body autonomy, our rights are all on the platform of revolution. These moments, quiet or loud, are the shift we are experiencing. How we ascend means how we flow with the bends, like music. How we prepare our minds without going all militia. How we feel gorgeous while allowing in the ugly. Each day, a drama is being played out, a new melody in the works. Our work is to grow with these moments, these vibrations, and our birthright is to expand and draw out the very best of ourselves and those around us.

I attempt to proceed forward in life with caution, humor, bravery, and openness. I am paying attention. I am not letting negativity rule me, as I do not consent to feed it. And I admit to having an agenda. Everyone has an agenda. I wish to be present to the opportunity to evolve as a servant, in love, in joy, and awake. I am trying not to be an asshole. But it happens.

Paramount to this process is the fact that I am manifesting at an immediate rate. What I say comes to fruition at an accelerated speed. How I used to manifest

over years now happens in minutes. This forces me to be incredibly mindful. I feel the responsibility of this power that I wield, this proprietary blend of influential manifestation. It has the capacity to be cutting as well as benevolent.

This manifestation endowment is not specific to me. Anyone can tap into the ability. But not everyone will. You are here, reading this. Obviously you are on the road to mastery as well. But what does that mean? What is it really to manifest? And how does the process begin?

Another valid query: is this professed ascension process one-way, or might it actually be both an ascending and descending practice?

If we are all living together on this planet, and breathing in the same air, we are also hearing the same sounds. At least we have access to it. We are also feeling the same energies, or at least we are all being introduced to them. There is so much negativity at our fingertips. Energetically it is being expelled out and upon us like garlic breath. It's intense. Higher and lower vibrational beings, somewhere on the spectrum of good and evil, are attempting to play us like puppets. Perhaps it is they who put people into power, so many levels up and down. Perhaps it is they who are whispering in our ears and minds. And who are they? Who has the power to set us moving in one direction psychologically, to split us ideologically? Who has the know-how to move us like cattle herd

towards their agenda? And does that mean they have the ability to tap into our very souls?

I don't deign to pretend to have any actual answers.

I do know, and this is way more important, that there is the positive higher level network of energy, matter, and soul being that extends beyond this material grid. I believe there are people that carry wisdom traditions so sacred, so old, and so much more powerful than their negative counterparts.

I believe in the light working warriors who are grounding in the higher vibratory and thus lower density energy for those who cannot. This service is part of the new science, tracked by government agencies and citizen researchers/alchemists alike. Take, for example, the dramatic transformation of the Schumann Resonance. The frequency of the planet is changing. Evidence of a new earth is all around us if only we have the eyes to see, ears to hear, and courage to share.

These souls and this primordial positive radiation are as real as can be. These bountiful and beautiful advanced civilized energies are coming through to help shepherd in our supreme joy, empathy, organization, and our most desired excellence as humans. Confidence, trust, cooperation. We can tap into all of this. We can choose it over negativity.

Of course, we can.

How much agency do we have to ride the waves the way we wish? Are we bobbing freely or are we being pushed down again and again. Are we simply talking to ourselves? Is the tape playing our own sad emotional wounds? Is it just trauma? Or is there more. Is there something higher happening in the ethers for us regular folk? What is the science of this, and how can we assume accountability and responsibility enough to be in both surrender and empowerment?

The sharing in this story is one of constantly asking these questions. It's a story about how to be in the driver's seat when you know your Subaru Outback is in the same lane as some flying Elon Musk free- energy mind controlled dealie.

We still have gas in 2020. Like all things in the material world, gas itself is a tool. It's just an example of what we still have as a natural resource. How it is used, how we choose to use it is on its own spectrum. Right now in 2020, we still own our own cars, our bodies, our religions, and our freedom. We still have the right and choice to use homeopathy over allopathic medicine. We have home birth which is to say natural birth, and we have hospital birth which is to say medical miracles. We have all the choice now. How to keep that choice while holding the knowledge that the advanced technology has already created the origin's doppleganger is a worthy footnote.

The manual for the yoga certification school I created and now run with my wonderful husband

Kalánidhi das begins with the Sanskrit line achintya-
bheda-abheda tattva. It means the truth of life is that
we and everything in it are inconceivably both one
and separate.

It's a both-and world. Notice the inconceivable
part. This is the very beginning, not the end, of
ascension. This is the softness of the mind that adheres
to the strength of faith. It takes both to ascend. It
takes wisdom and devotion. It takes the ability to
understand the individual and the community. It takes
boots on the ground with pristine psychic agility. It
means to become one with your personal greatness
while understanding your fallibility. And it goes way
beyond your physical prowess, healthy brain function,
dealing with trauma.

Beyond trauma, story and habitual patterns, we
have to dig deeper. By becoming quieter and simpler
in the mind, we grow into our heart-center, where the
soul resides, and thus believe as we embody the truth
that there is more than we know.

That practice is called Surrender.

For most of us on the ascension path, we will
not pass this level. Why? Because in surrender, we
recognize that we are not the Creator, Maintainer, and
Destroyer. We are not the Controller. We have free
will, but we also have destiny. And if this is true, we
are unique sparks of whatever is more powerful and
bountiful than us. And that means there is something,

whether you call it the cosmic creation, source, divinity, goddess, higher- consciousness, alien, other-worldly beings, or any other name. There needs to be some source of wisdom, power, blessings, bounty, beauty, or any other divine attribute that we are ascending towards.

And while that source has personality, while she/he/it is perhaps a person on some timeline, we are made of it. Some reverence must be there, in us and from us. Some tiny humble surrender in the heart.

That is the hardest part, the giving up of complete dominance while empowering oneself and one's community to employ qualification. Difficult does not begin to describe the life-long challenge of giving up our narrative, our programming. We are born into that programming. In every mushy moment from birth to maybe seven, we are literally recalling the actual being our nature, as well as adapting our nurture. We adults are fierce if not determined about our beliefs.

And we grip.

This is how we have gotten to the degraded painful situation we are in today. We would be blind to not admit how serious the situation is in our climate. Perhaps you are totally happy and peaceful, and that is so awesome. Keep it going, stay high! But you are reaching and yearning, are you not? You desire more peace, more beauty, more sweetness perhaps.

We want more. We want more Love.

And so comes in the recognition that 2020 needs to be something new, because the old must come down for the new to come in — a new earth, a new globe, a new leadership, and a new program.

If it is true that there are cycles, and that this new millenia is sherpa-ing in a new way in the material realm, then the old ways are completely coming down. We are talking about government, law, medicine, art, music, and education. We are talking about the blowing of folks' minds.

This could be shattering, as the veil of illusion comes down, and some of our favorite people go down with it. We already know that the depths of secret negative forces are not so secret anymore. Every topic we do not wish to see, hear, feel or discuss is coming to the surface. And no one will be able to escape it, because we let it in. We allowed all of it into our lives in the most personal way. Our smart devices radiating on top of our very skin, to the 5G towers on every street lamp in Los Angeles (and growing in some of the worlds most ecologically rich lands). We have handed over our daily existence, our secret hopes, fears and desires over to the 'powers that be' and they have utilized our energy as a resource.

This is not new. This has happened but not as extreme for many thousands of years.

Astrological science shows us where we are going, what could happen, and what we might prepare for. It's good! Or at least, it can be. But these negative forces are the stronghold of old evil, and it will not go away easily. Good is as strong as evil. And now is not the time to lay down our life over to group consensus sans real science, secrets, lies, people we have never met, psychologies we don't really believe in, programs that want to dominate, unnecessary policing of our lives, or narratives that suit the lowest-class needs of our animal nature without addressing our high-class needs of the spirit's truth.

Just the opposite. It's a good time to wake the eff up and be awesome.

Surrender is the giving over of one's preciousness. Surrender is of one's heart and soul to something absolutely fantastic, beyond this world, beyond the third, fourth, and fifth generations, grids, and dimensional realms. We surrender to something more than otherworldly, to divinity itself.

What if we surrender to grace itself, auspiciousness herself, beauty himself. What if we were to step into our new roles, as masters of our lower vibrations, knighted and delegated by all that is positive. So what if we give over our programming — what could happen, we die? What dies? Our emotional baggage? Our pain? Our psyche?

I have had the incredible privilege of experiencing

psychologically and physically debilitating pain for my entire life. Chronic migraines are not a simple karma, they take over the entire being because they are in our brain. Our brain is the key to all communication in our body. If your brain is on fire, your brain stem misaligned, and your cervical vertebrae out of place, nothing really feels awesome.

The work it takes to go deep within, when I cannot escape, is a life path I wouldn't wish on anyone in this way. There are countless more dangerous and difficult karmic offerings. But this pain is my life path. I believe I chose it. I believe I have been doing this soul mapping thing for many lifetimes.

I am kind of done with this migraine incarnation. Not with the work, but with the specific symptom(s). I believe the ascension is that I am now able to do my subconscious journey work that I am so clearly built for, in a conscious way. The dream mastery that shines as one of the main emblems of my life is now a daily, waking moment practice. Awake, eyes open or closed, I am living my mastery. And I am ascending out of pain. The work has begun, again, as it does in cycles. I am in surrender. And I will stay in surrender as I progress. Not perfect, it is progress. Progress in ascension.

Jane Sloven

Writer. Healer. Creator.

J ane Sloven is a writer, healer, creator and co-
leader of contemplative and healing worship, semi-
retired clinical social worker, and fully retired attorney
and mediator. A graduate of A Society of Souls, trained
in non-dual Kabbalistic Healing, Jane has re-entered that
four-year training twenty-three years after graduating. As
she approaches her 70th birthday, Jane is studying energy
healing with Deborah King, learning from empath and
healer Wendy De Rosa, finalizing the sequel to her mystery,
Termination of Benefits, and painting landscapes good
enough to hang on the walls of her own home. She enjoys
loving her extraordinary husband, her wonderful friends,
her unruly extended family, her fabulous god-daughters, her
fuzzy dog, and her gardens—planted and cared for by her
husband. Some of Jane's favorite pastimes are sipping tea
with friends, reading novels, wearing feathered, flowered
hats, cooking, and indulging in uncontrollable laughter.

www.JaneSloven.com

Musings on Mortality

"Don't look over there," Dee said, but I'd already seen the tall man with the gray face slumped in the phone booth. I remember the hush, then voices, sirens, an ambulance, a stretcher.

"What's wrong with him?" I asked.

"He's dead, honey. But don't you worry about it," Dee said. But I did worry. I worried about who was waiting for that man at home. I understood the consequences, even then.

That was my first encounter with the mystery of death. It took place in a grocery store. For years, I thought I was seven at the time, but I must have been quite a bit younger because I remember my legs dangling from the shopping cart as our housekeeper filled it with groceries. The memory that remains clear is the tall man with the gray face in the phone booth.

✳ ✳ ✳ ✳ ✳

My ancestors were Eastern European Jews. The Holocaust cast a long shadow throughout my childhood. My grandmother grieved for her family, murdered in their Polish village. In America, what killed us was the diet—meat, potatoes, sour cream, chicken fat, sugar, and stress—causing fatal heart attacks or strokes. Both my grandfathers died before my birth. Grandma Luba, seventy-four, died from a heart attack. I was eleven. Grandma Jeanette died at eighty-one from the effects of a stroke. I was thirteen.

Yet they felt close when I caught the scent of their perfume, remembered the feel of their soft cheeks, the love in their encircling arms.

Death was sudden, frightening, and inescapable. I knew bodies lay in caskets, but where did souls go? What did I sense when I felt loved ones near?

My family attended synagogue regularly. I couldn't describe what I felt there, but I thought it must be God, beaming in through the sanctuary's stained glass windows scattering rainbows on the floor, the melodies of Hebrew prayers.

When I was eleven, my father had his first heart attack. He was forty-eight. A handsome, prematurely gray, blue-eyed man, he managed and co-owned a lumber yard. His shirt pockets held sharpened pencils. He smelled of Old Spice and freshly sawn lumber. While he was hospitalized, I was terrified he'd die. I walked through my neighborhood, knowing the fieldstone houses, tall trees, and green lawns were not as solid as they appeared. The ground could disappear at any moment.

❖ ❖ ❖ ❖ ❖

I began college in D.C., a year after Martin Luther King and Bobby Kennedy's assassination. I studied, dated, and protested the Vietnam War, passing tanks and soldiers holding rifles. My campus was tear-gassed. Nothing felt safe; nothing felt normal. My terrified parents wanted me home.

That summer, my burgeoning independence

precipitated such conflict that my parents sent me to California, hoping my cousin Marsha could intervene. An intense dread led me to cut the trip short and fly home the Wednesday before Labor Day. Thursday was hot and muggy. My father played golf, my parents hosted a dinner party. My father didn't mention chest pain. He went to work Friday, called my mother at noon. She picked him up, brought him home, called his cardiologist, and drove him to the hospital. I opened a medical dictionary for 'Coronary Thrombosis.' The words, *"Usually followed by sudden death,"* leaped off the page.

I saw my father for five minutes on Sunday. He lay amid a tangle of tubes in the ICU. His face was gray. I held his hand, said I loved him. That night, I slept beside my mother. She shook me awake at 4:45, Monday morning, Labor Day.

"I had a nightmare," she said. "A bird bit off the head of a turtle." Birds were harbingers of death in our family. The hospital called a minute or two later.

I shattered—no ground, no light, no holiness. Fragile but functioning, I finished college, moved to Boston, went to law school, moved to Maine. I met my husband at a workshop on Therapeutic Touch. We paired up to sense each other's energy fields. Romance followed, long walks, long talks, much laughter. We married a year later. He completed medical school. I completed a Master's in Social Work. It was a time of healing, repair.

We joined a Reform synagogue. The worship services, melodies, and warm community brought me once again into that indefinable closeness with my ancestors.

One summer, we stayed on Cape Cod in an old Inn. Angry male voices woke me up in the night. I shook Joe awake.

"There are two ghosts in the hall. Old sea captains. They keep throwing each other down the stairs but end up back on the landing, doing it over and over."

Joe couldn't hear or see them, but the following day when I told the Innkeepers, they refunded our money.

We spent a year trying to get pregnant. When a home test was finally positive, my GP examined me. He said something looked wrong; the embryo might have lodged in my fallopian tube instead of my uterus. He suggested immediate testing, saying if the tube burst, I could die. My nationally known holistic gynecologist examined me the next day. "An early pregnancy," she said. "No need for tests." We chose her forecast.

Ten days later, excruciating pain flung me to my knees. I stumbled down two flights of stairs in my apartment. My landlady drove me to the hospital.

A Johnny, a gurney, an IV. I was whisked from here to there, an ultrasound, an X-ray, I'm not sure. My focus was on a different experience, a luminous space where spirituality, sensation, and ordinary reality dissolve. My spirit left my body, hovering nearby, intermittently slipping back inside, where pain and urgency exaggerated the smell of antiseptic, the intensity of bright lights. Joe arrived and held my hand. The surgeon introduced himself.

"I don't mean to be controlling," I said, "but you

need to get me into the operating room. I keep leaving my body, and I'm not sure how many more times I can get back in."

He seemed stunned, asked if it would be okay to feel my belly first.

"Yes. But we don't have much time," I said.

He apparently agreed because I was swiftly wheeled into and out of an elevator to the operating room. A nurse held my hand. I vomited into a silver pan. Darkness descended. Awareness returned like an island floating in and out of clouds — a bed beside a window, Joe sleeping in a chair, holding my hand. Pain. A smiling male nurse with a syringe.

My recuperation was lengthy. The surgeon became my gynecologist. Tests showed a congenitally deformed fallopian tube. I was infertile. Grief compounded grief. Love, friendships, worship, books on Jewish mysticism, and the chanting of Hebrew prayers sustained me. I eventually moved on, renting a cottage with two women for our counseling offices.

❀ ❀ ❀ ❀ ❀

That summer, twitching, flashing lights, and floating circles interrupted my meditations. I painted what I felt — a golden zigzag emanating light rays atop a rectangle surrounded by blue circles — a view of the operating room from above. The blue circles — surgical caps on the doctors and nurses. The golden zigzag — my essence.

The veil between worlds became porous. As I laid in a hammock, my father appeared, showing movies of happy times in his life. I understood it was time to focus on life's pleasures. I'm a skeptic and a mystic but had no doubt about that encounter.

Joe and I entered a healing school based on Kabbalah and Buddhism. I received healings from the founder. During one, while I was in Maine and he in New Jersey, I felt my legs fill with pink liquid. Afterward, for the first time in years, the ground beneath my feet felt solid. I fully inhabited my body. I felt stronger, more confident. How can any of us explain these experiences taking place in a realm we don't usually inhabit?

Joe and I honed intuitive skills, connected with sacred essences from our mystical tradition. The skeptic in me wondered if the class was in a mass trance. We may have been— trance states are often part of healing work. But I knew we weren't delusional about the realms of light we entered, inhabited by invisible but palpable beings. And the healings were real.

A close friend's father was in a Midwest hospital on life support. She asked for our help. Under our teacher's supervision, I became a proxy for her father. The life force in my body felt almost extinguished. Joe asked diagnostic questions. To respond, I struggled up from what felt like the bottom of a muddy pond. My voice was low and slow, my limbs incapable of movement. I was happy to disconnect once we knew the right healings. We did them daily until my friend's father recovered and said rabbis interrupted his sleep, asking him to eat golden Hebrew letters.

I created contemplative and healing services for my synagogue. Poetry, prayer, melody, and silence

opened gates to the sacred. In my counseling practice, clinical hypnosis and trauma-treatment techniques allowed me to witness inexplicable resilience and recovery. During healings, I felt like a bird, flying over vast expanses. Sacred space enveloped me and my clients.

My mother was diagnosed with ovarian cancer. After an eight-hour surgery, I stood by her bedside in the ICU. No one else saw the man on the other side of her bed before he disappeared. That night I found him in my mother's photo album. It comforted me to know her grandfather was beside her.

During the last ten days of her life, I cared for my mother with my brother, cousin, friend, and hospice. One night intense energy filled her room. I witnessed veils parting, heard she would simply discard the husk of her body.

I've retired. Covid arrived. I'm studying energy healing, offering long-distance sessions to friends and classmates. Guides work through my hands. By now, I should trust the help of guides, guardians, and loved ones on the other side—yet I'm often mystified. What I do know is this: *We are beings of light who make a home, for a time, in our bodies.*

Kiana Love

Artist. Creatrix. Wild Woman.

Kiana Love is the founder of Be Wild Woman. She is an energy healer who helps overwhelmed women and survivors of childhood trauma feel safe and loved, so they can trust themselves, find freedom in their bodies, and enjoy their lives. Kiana's teachings and work lead women to the understanding that when a woman begins to trust herself, she learns the answers to questions she is seeking are already inside of her. As a result, they begin to have more peace of mind and freedom to be themselves. They are empowered to feel confident, creative, curious, are filled with courage to speak their truth, ask for what they want—and get it— each and every day! Kiana holds a B.S. in Behavioral Science from the University of Houston, and has certifications in somatic healing and holistic health. She is a Wild Woman Healer, Reiki Master, Integrated Energy Therapy Instructor, Vortex Healer, Intuitive, Holistic Health Counselor, Herbalist, Reflexologist, Interfaith Minister and Yoga Teacher.

www.BeWildWoman.com

Wild Woman Speaks:

The following pages are channeled healing message via art and words from Wild Woman through Kiana Love.

POWER OF LIFE

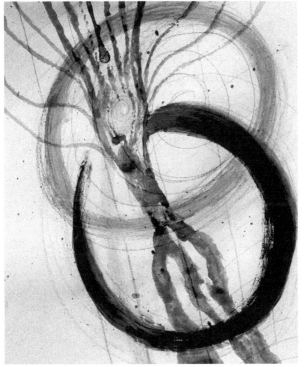

I am the power of life within you.
    I do not need words;
    I simply am.

    Words are not meaning:
    Feeling is;
    Being is.

Words can only approximate
what IS here in your gut:

Visceral Life.

I cannot be contained in your or
anyone else's words.

Expand your awareness beyond the
chatter of your mind.

Surrender to the soul intelligence of
your blood.

Let it flow free;
Set Yourself Free.

Fuck the words.

Break free of your prison.
You cannot be contained by words.

You are life.
Feel me here & you will know it is
so.

CYST TALKS WITH WILD WOMAN

Cyst: I am my cyst and I feel complete.
I feel heavy, bursting with life that
wants to flow free.

Cyst to me: I am my cyst and I need release.
I need freedom to flow.

Wild Woman: This breath is the wave
you've been waiting for.
Freedom is here.
Power is here.
I am here in your breath.

Set yourself free to feel me here.

Surrender to the tide, wild wave of love
flowing through you.

This is a daily sacred dialogue with my
paraovarian cyst and Wild Woman.

Wild Woman, our instinctive
feminine nature and life force
speaks through us and to us in all
that we experience.
Here she is as I experience her in
my daily healing practice with her.

This reminds me that the ocean is right
here in me. It reminds me that I can
trust it and surrender to it.

I love this wave! It makes me hungry for
the ocean; for Hawaii my favorite
place on the planet where my heart
is home, for Venezuela where I spent
my teen years near the beach,
and for Brighton Beach
and Coney Island just a 15 minute
bike ride from home.
Mama Ocean, Nature is calling.
Let's catch a wave today...this one,
this breath. Inhale, exhale.

MENSTRUAL MUSINGS
(Day One)

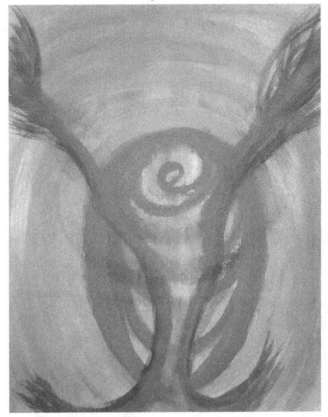

Dear Woman,

Behold your inner temple, womb to vulva, egg to baby, desires to creation manifest. Each and every one of you is a creatrix. It is here in your organs reflected. It is in your actions, your emotions and in your soul. Being a woman, with female organs, is no more and no less sacred than that of any other variation of biology. All are sacred expressions of wildness.

I am here to guide you to experience your sacred wild feminine nature manifest. Only then can you as a soul, as a nation, as a people, as a being come together into divine union.

> All of you is wild
> All of you is sacred.
> Worship at the temple of your soul.
> Revere life.
> Be Wild.
> Inhale, exhale.

MENSTRUAL MUSINGS
(Day Two)

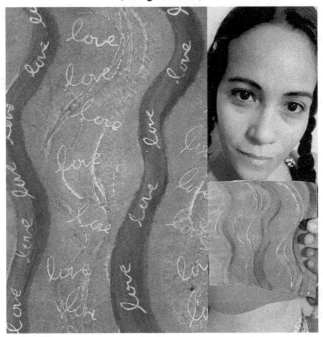

Dear Woman,

There is only love here in your blood. Let all else be washed away as your lining releases. Let go of the world and surrender to the infinite in you. Listen deeply to your heart beat, your breath, your longing. All is sacred. This is your music. Let your body move with your music. Set yourself free and dance with me.

I Wild Woman have spoken.
Daily channeled healing message from Her to you:

It's day 2 of my Menstrual Cycle. After my morning practice of rooting with Wild Woman and honoring the wild sacred in me, I ask her to flow through me, to speak and heal women and the world through me. I paint and write when I feel Her energy and presence flowing through me.

She has asked me to share these pieces with you to awaken you to experience the joy of being wild. She wants you to know that you are Nature so that you can experience peace and joy.

She wants us all to awaken to the sacredness of the feminine and the masculine. She says that in order for us to experience wholeness we need both. We need to heal the feminine to heal the masculine.

I paint with my blood when I bleed to honor it as sacred life. I do this publicly even though some of you may feel disturbed or even revolted by it.

> I do it even though there is a part of me that wants everyone to like me and no one to judge me.

> I do it because I am dedicated to healing the feminine and ending violence against the feminine.

I do it because I know what is like to grow up with painful, debilitating cycles, thinking it's awful to be a woman.

I thought God made a mistake making me a girl.

I do it because listening to my body and to Wild Woman I realize how sacred my menstrual blood and my reproductive organs are...and how blessed I am to be a woman.
I do it for the woman or man that needs to know they and the woman they were born through is sacred.

We need to know and feel
the sacredness of life
in order to revere
and delight in
living.

I do this because I desire a world where we can all celebrate and experience the joy of living together.

I dream of this today and hope
you'll join me.

Leana Kriel

Metaphysicist. Counsellor. Teacher and Student.

D r. Leana Kriel – PhD has been working as a Coaching Professional since 1998. She specializes in helping people identify and achieve their personal goals by coping with the issues that are causing them distress, anxiety, and stress. Her areas of expertise include Career Coaching, Relationship Coaching and Life Coaching. The overarching goal of Leana's work is to guide clients to create lives where their minds, bodies and souls are in balance. She is a lifelong student who encourages her clients to grow and live their best lives. Leana resides in South Africa and takes great pride in the progress and success of her clients.

www.DrLeanaKriel.com

Calling the Goddess
Within into Power

Background:

As we grow spiritually or if spirt is doing its level best to move you toward a space where you start to do some introspection, that is a good and healthy place to be. I am sure we are all aware that change is normally rather uncomfortable and can be somewhat scary. Instead of change, I like to think that when we align with our authentic self, we shed the people, places and situations in our life that do not resonate with our evolution.

Interestingly everything and everyone that does not serve your highest good will generally leave your space as you start and progress on your journey.

Understand that as absolutely wonderful and spiritual as this may sound, it comes with very real feelings, some of them will make you smile, laugh and enforce absolute joy while others will break your heart, rip open wounds you forgot you had and ego will twist your mind into giving it all up for the mundane and average to make sure you settle for everything you do not want.

A review of yourself and your world:

So how do you start your journey to self-discovery and authenticity? Well, I believe that it is different for each of us. Most often you will start to question either what you know to be true or your current reality. This a good thing! Part of your own spiritual evolution will most likely involve a review of your life as you know it, which should if you are being brutally honest lead to an amazing spiritual journey.

One of the very wonderful things I have learned on my journey is that spirit and spiritual journey has nothing to do with religion – for me anyway. I grew up in a very religious family and remember most of the time that I was sitting in church my only question was "is this it?" Is what happens in life all disconnected and linked to whether I come to church or not, if I pray or not, ect …..sure most of you will know what I'm getting at……I made some very interesting choices in my life and have been very blessed on all my different routes I travelled, even when they did not go my way or was not necessarily in my best interest or for my highest good at the time.

I have come to learn that the intent with which we do and say things has a very direct impact on the outcome. I believe it is imperative to control your own mind and thoughts. Know that the ONLY person you can change is you and the only control you will ever

have is over yourself. Please do not ever live in the illusion that you can change any other person, Hun you will cry and be angry every day for the rest of your life! Seriously, not your husband, children or boyfriend, no one!! Stick to living your best life and being the best version of you, that is all you can control and change and quite frankly it is your *responsibility* to do so.

So, time to take a serious look at your life and then move inward as you do. Take a look at what you do for a living. Is what you are doing making you happy, puts a smile on your face, allows you a good night's sleep? If you are doing nothing to generate an income, what do you do that gives you joy or happiness – taking care of your family is not part of this list – if you have a family you do this automatically, you're a magnificent woman I'll expect nothing less!

This is about you and for you ONLY. If your employment is not your happy place, we need to work on changing it. Do you know what your dream job is? If so what do you need to get it? Perhaps you need some additional studies, experience or just apply. Remember and know without a doubt that if it is meant for you it will be yours. The Universe expects that you take action towards your own dreams and desires, so that they can rush to assist and guide you where needed. If you are not doing anything, why not, what would you love to do, what have you always dreamed of doing? Once you have these answers you will be able to put a plan together on how and what to do in order for you to follow your dream.

If you happen to have a spouse that "prohibits" you from following your dream in any way, may it be by negatively speaking about your abilities, a general decline in your dream or just expecting you to be home, well that in itself should be an answer to many of your questions and hopefully you will be in a position to turn this around for yourself. Sometimes our partners need a reminder of the very powerful goddesses that each of us carry inside, the magnificent and very capable woman that we are! If they happen to be scared straight, well now, that is on them! :)

Then move on to - if you want to share your life with someone, if you already do then perhaps you want to take some time to evaluated your relationship. This is rather difficult especially in the beginning because generally challenging the current status quo is very unsettling. I suggest that you have a general overview as to your dream person and how your life currently compares. Perhaps you already know of a few little things you would like to change ie: sex life or emotional attentiveness. Make a suggestion or two on how you can better this for the both of you. Often the fact that we do not talk about taboo subjects is part of the problem. Luckily you are a goddess, the result, you have built-in all you will ever need, irrespective if you believe yet or not.

Move through your home, does it make you happy, is this where you want to be? What does your

perfect home look like and what do you need to do to live in it? So I am a firm believer that the universe need to be able to trust you with what you already have first. So you may have a small little spot to live in and your dream is a mansion somewhere on a hill... what does your small spot look like? Is it clean, well-taken care of, grass cut, walls clean and painted every couple of years, are the cupboards tidy, clean floors and kitchen? If not perhaps you want to start there, you can't have a beautiful life, if what you have does not resemble that which you desire. *FYI, the same is true for your body image!*

If you would like to have a fit body, then you will have to be mindful of what you put into it and how you treat it. I teach my daughter that her body hears every word she thinks and says about herself, what is your message? You can make very small but consistent changes to renew your mind and body and your internal dialogue. Please be kind to yourself, you are all you have.

Sample Questions:

Remember that you start small, these changes are for you. They are not to hurt or damage anyone else, my goodness that is Karma you cannot afford, I promise you. Be honest with yourself. You can just focus on one question at a time. If you do not instinctively have an answer it is ok. All that means is that you need to spend some time with yourself. Do

this by taking a 30 min bath alone - take the dog for a walk - leave to collect the kids 10 minutes earlier so you can just breath, switch off the radio in the car – get up 15 minutes earlier in the morning have coffee or tea or juice alone in your garden or wherever there is some form of nature (a pot plant will also do).
The answer will come to you.

> Below are some questions that you can ask yourself for guidance and clarity.
> - What do I want to do?
> - What do I want to feel (physical and emotional) like when I do this?
> - What does this look like?
> - What does it smell like?
> - What does it taste like?
> - Who do I want to share my life with?
> - What does sharing my life feel like with this person?
> - What does my life look like with this person?
> - Do I want to share my life with anyone?
> - Do I want children?
> - Where do I want to live?
> - What do I want my home to look, smell and feel like?

For the best outcomes I would look at the answers every 6 months and answer them again, some will stay the same and some will have to be changed a little. As you go on this journey you will notice that you are confronted with things you never even thought off

when you started your path because they were not an option or they were not in your purview.

Angel, you may have forgotten who you are, but your inner goddess and guides have not! Listen to the Magnificent women in you for guidance to a beautiful life, you are enough, you are good enough and you deserve a beautiful life regardless of what you have been told.

Rise goddesses you are needed!

Melissa Kennedy

Angel Channel. Empath. Psychic Cowgirl.

Rev. Melissa Kennedy, known as the Psychic Cowgirl, is first and foremost a healer. She firmly believes that in connecting with our divine spark, healing begins to unfold in our lives. She truly believes that all Intuitive work with her clients is healing on some level. Every session is infused with divine light and love. She is attuned to many different healing modalities Including Reiki and Atlantean Healing. Melissa embodies all the Clairs, ie: clairvoyance (clear seeing); clairaudience (clear hearing); clairsentience(clear feeling); claircognizance (clear knowing); clairgustance (clear tasting); clairalience (clear smelling). Drawing on these, along with her empath abilities and her educational background in Metaphysical Science, she works together with clients for their highest and best good, in this now moment in time.

www.WhisperingWindPsychicCowgirl.com

Midnight:

A LOVE STORY

In a world that seems to hold so much Darkness. There is always light, there is always hope. Love always finds a way. Love is the most enduring of all emotions. It is always right there, below the surface, buried deep, sometimes as we gently unearth its light, we see the beauty in its flaws. The unfolding of the enduring spirit, that resides in the hearts of all living beings.

When we open our hearts to love in all of its forms, in all of its creation, in all of its materialization in every embodiment, in every gesture of peace and kindness. It is then that all mankind and the creatures of the earth will become one in this beautiful dance of life. Love flows like a fountain with no end, always keep your heart open to its truest, purest, and unexpected sources.

This is a story about love, it is the embodiment of love, in every sense of the word and all that resides in the very recesses of its very manifestations here in our world, in our hearts, and minds. Love is the light that lives, it burns so bright, it glows from the inside out, despite any darkness.

The year of 2020 has been a borage of every kind of human emotion. It has been a test to the human

psyche, the human mind, and our enduring spirit, that prevails, even in the midst of uncertainty, fear, and the unknown.

This is a story about a Black Cat that seemingly appeared from out of nowhere, totally lost, afraid, and neglected. A Black Cat that clearly had been given the short end of life's stick. Yet, when our eyes met, I knew he would be mine.

A month before Midnight had miraculously appeared from behind some bushes at my farm, I had been thinking, *I really need a black cat!* It had been years since I had one. I am talking, for many years. I was probably 8 years old, the last time I had a black cat. I am a grown woman now, my children are grown as well, so that will give you an idea of just how long it has been.

I will add that this entire process, with the appearance of Midnight in my life, has reconnected me to my youth in more ways than I can list. The most beautiful thought that occurred to me, in the building of our relationship is; *Midnight made me feel like I was 8 years old again.* He ignited that pure, innocent love, of a child's heart, that wanted so badly to let him know, that life is not as cruel as it had been handed to him, up until this point of our meeting. His appearance ignited within me, the flame of pure, innocent intention, of unconditional love.

My heart, my soul, my entire being, was calling

out to his battered little heart and soul. I think I needed a friend more than he did. I think I needed to feel hope, I needed to feel triumph over tragedy, I needed to experience unconditional love and healing.

It has since come to me, that Midnight was the only thing that could have ever restored my hope, my innocence, my enduring spirit to give love, and receive love, in its purest of forms.

Animals have that gift, no human being can ever seem to measure up. We are so flawed in our form of love for each other. I often ponder, what would my life be without all of the beautiful animals I have had the pleasure of having in my life, up until this point? There are seemingly, countless, that have helped me understand and experience that bond between animal and human, that magical bond of unconditional love. To the observer, there seems to be no dialogue at all between the two beings.

I can assure you, the language of the heart, is speaking volumes at any given moment. Communication happens without words, even between human beings. We are energy, embodied. We give it off, we receive it in all interactions and with all beings. Our vibration, our energy signature even impacts our own spaces where we live and dwell. When we vibrate at the highest frequencies of love, I think love is brought to us, right when we need it most.

We just have to be open to every manifestation of

this love, in our physical reality!

Midnight, though he was skittish, malnourished and full of fear, anxiety and trauma, somehow felt my vibration of love, that I had been sending out, manifesting it back to me. I had been telling some friends prior to Midnight's appearance that I really wanted a black cat! Then shortly after my verbal expression of my desire for a black cat in my life. I had a dream of a beautiful black cat.

For me, this is not unusual because what I am manifesting in my life will appear to me in the dream state. I then told a friend I had a dream about a beautiful black cat and once again I said that I really needed a black cat in my life and I would really like to get one but, since I already had three cats at the farm, I just could not justify getting another one.

I mean, at this time I already had four horses, two French Bulldogs, three cats, and a gaggle of chickens! How could I justify getting another cat? My husband would be like, oh no, here she goes again! I did not want to even tell him, I wanted a black cat! Though he has been super enabling, as far as supporting my enduring love for saving every stray I can find. I just could not tell him my new hearts desire was a Black Cat!

Not too long after I had the dream of the beautiful black cat, this same cat appeared to me psychically! I had a clairvoyant vision of him. His eyes were the most mesmerizing golden eyes I had ever seen!

I was like, okay Universe, you are playing with me! It was not a week later, after his clairvoyant vision that Midnight appeared in my yard! He was hiding behind some bushes and peered out at me after my sweet little temptress, Mittens walked out from the very spot he had appeared! There is no doubt she brought him home! He followed her, I mean, everyone is looking for love, and sometimes in all the wrong places! But, not this time!

My heart literally leaped with joy!! I could hardly believe it, there was my Black Cat!

When our eyes Met, it was love at first sight! It was the kind of eye locking moment that you realize, there is work up ahead, there is a lot of healing that is going to have to take place but, the love is there, behind the eyes of fear, the light struck me, like a flash.

There was never any doubt that I would be able to tame him down, and show him that love, hope and a family was his. He just had to work with me. I had plenty of time. I mean what else do you have to do during a pandemic? It took me nearly a month to be able to reach out and pat Midnight. I would feed him special canned chicken. It is amazing what canned chicken can do to win the heart of a starving, petrified cat.

The first time I gently touched him, he bolted. It

was progress, yet my heart hurt, because I know how badly he had been treated. Gradually, as the days progressed, Midnight would come out of the brush where he slept, at the sound of my voice, calling him by name. I could see the delight in his eyes, that someone cared enough to call him by name, and he happily obliged by being very vocal back and he would eventually, slowly approach me.

I would sit on the end of my open horse trailer, and feed him there every day. I kept a routine. I gradually moved the food dish closer to me every time I would feed him. He would position himself so his tail would touch my leg as he ate his food. I could tell, he just loved that little bit of human contact.

We then got to a place where I could pat him, and eventually, he would just come up to me, brush against my legs, and welcome me to his yard! It just made my heart happy. Every time he brushed against my legs, I could feel the love, and clearing energy, he was returning the favor of my kindness ten fold, and if there was ever a time I needed clearing, it was right now, in this train wreck I call 2020!

We gradually moved from outside spaces of contact to the interior of the barn, again, this took time for Midnight to feel safe in a closed space, even though I had the barn door wide open. I would sit in my chair, and my next goal was to have him sit in my lap. This too eventually happened. When it did, once again my adult heart was replaced with the pure

love and innocence of a child's heart! His body was so warm as he sat in my lap, it was then that I figured out, Midnight was a natural healer.

I know the energy signature of a healer, as I am one myself. The first time he jumped in my lap, I could feel the warmth of his unconditional love, my entire body was filled with the heat from his healing energy and love! It was so warm, it felt like I was having a hot flash! Then when he finally decided he had been in my lap long enough, when he jumped off, the bottom half of my body went weak.

You know that feeling, of your very first kiss, your first true love, when your knees get weak? That is the love Midnight gifted me with! Once again, I was like a young girl again! What an amazing spirit, what an amazing gift Midnight has been! My next goal is to make him my office cat. We have been working on getting him comfortable inside of the house. His trust in me, allows him to overcome his fear of being trapped inside.

It is such a good feeling to know that he now looks to me, a kind human, for safety. I look forward to so many more milestones with Midnight, and I know, he will go down as one of the most enduring love stories of my entire life. We truly have a bond that transcends space and time.

There is no doubt in my mind, Midnight and I have been together through many lifetimes. He is without a

doubt, a familiar. To me his appearance in my life, at this perfect moment in time for me, is proof of how the Universe is always working on our behalf. We just have to have the heart and mind of a child. We can never stop believing in miracles. We can never stop believing that we deserve them!

Keep dreaming, keep manifesting all of your hearts desires! If you want a Black CAT! Go and adopt one! Black cats have had a stigma attached to them. Trust me, the love you will receive from a black cat, is Magical, and Mystical in all ways that are good for the soul! I don't know about you but, I personally enjoy the Mystical and Magical things that life has to offer us! I am open to it all, even in the form of a Wayward, and once lost Soul, that I call Midnight.

Midnight You Have Found Your Place In This Crazy Year 2020 Peace to all, human and animals alike.

As you can see, my dream came to full fruition! Midnight is a much Loved house cat, and my healing support cat! He heals me, while I heal others! xo

As a side note: To all of the people out there
that are open to all things unexplained, and not yet
embraced by the masses - Midnight has been with
me in this lifetime, he was that cat I spoke of, from
my earlier years (In that incarnation with me, he was
tragically hit by a car, it was my first devastating loss,
I will never forget it).

My Brother and I both stayed home from School the next day. We had lost our first family member. Midnight has also appeared to me clairvoyantly, wearing the cutest little golden crown. He is truly an ascended, higher being. (AS are most cats, or dare I say all cats)! We also shared a life in Egypt. He was actually a cat being, like you see in the Egyptian hieroglyphics. Half man, half cat.

He has shown me images of what we looked like together in that lifetime. So amazing, he has also shown me some pyramids with ancient writing on them, rising up from the earth. The pyramid is covered in moss, and as it rises above the surface of the earth, the moss disappears and the pyramid becomes dark black in color with purple and green ancient writing. I can't wait to see what else Midnight has to share with me. He is truly a deep and soulful being!

Mika Leone

Healer. Teacher. Friend.

Mika Leone-Pettit M. Msc. is a wellness practitioner and spiritual teacher. She has 24 years of experience in the health and wellness industry and combines several modern and ancient techniques to energetically work with her clients to figure their unique wiring for the best outcomes and use of their potential. She has a Bachelors in Natural Health Studies from Clayton College of Natural Health and a Masters in Metaphysics from the University of Metaphysics. She is a doctoral student in Transpersonal Counseling at the University of Sedona. She helped open *The Gateway Metaphysical Gifts & Bookshop* in Los Angeles in 2013 and has been doing spiritual counseling and reading sessions since 2012. Her podcast, ***How To Heal*** focuses on combining practical health and spiritual knowledge that is easy to utilize in daily life. Along with teaching and spiritual counseling, Mika writes for *Herberia & Plant Healer's Magazine*. Her other offerings are classes, courses, online communities and ceremonies.

www.MikaLeone.com

Transforming The Mind
in a Chaotic World
(Excerpts from forthcoming book by Mika Leone-Pettit M.Msc.)

The Cosmic Ocean

When searching for truths of life and our existence, we must go beyond the five senses which are very limited. If physical existence through your senses and what can be experienced in this physical plane is the only connection you have to being alive, this limits your possibilities on many levels. Life gets murky and unclear quickly on how to manage it for the best outcomes.

We must enter the unseen levels and frequencies of the metaphysical which follows the cycles and flow of the cosmic ocean. In order for us to navigate this purely energetic all en-composing place of all forms of energy that never dies but instead transform, we must be as fluid and changing. With the right alignment, we can swim, float, dive or be carried by its waves to the experiences that align with our purpose.

Just as an apple seed has the potential to become a beautiful tree that produces an abundance of fruit or gifts to share with the world, we are seeds ourselves at conception with limitless potential to create and add to

the conscious collective. When we learn our personal energetic wiring, we can find our inner still point and swim the cosmic ocean with grace and gratitude for our experiences.

Swimming The Cosmic Ocean

Treacherous tides of chaos cannot
contain my truth,
For I am everywhere & beyond.
I weave my knowledge into the fabric
of all being,
With glorious purpose & relentless resolve;
For I am spirit here to evolve.

Smile, Flow & Let Go

The method of smiling, feeling the flow and letting go was a life changing experience for me. It set me on a course that allowed me to stay happily on my spiritual path. I created this poem to help me put things in to perspective along my journey. It helps me to understand I am a spirit having an experience and to not hold too tightly to the illusions of the physical world and the ego. It reminds me to just let go and I will be guided on my journey through this life. I hope it inspires you to create your own guidance that resonates with your practice.

If I Let Go

I was born of illusion
With a veil too thick to penetrate
Though truth has always been within
I could not see
Do I need to
If I let go
My spirit is always searching & seeking
My ego is always on guard
For if I let go
Where is ego's home
Its perceived throne
As the journey continues & never ends
It changes many courses with twists & bends
I now understand
I now see
The light was always a part of me
If I let go

Quieting The Mind Ritual & Meditation

I work a lot in the unseen realms with energy, colors, sounds, imagery, mantras, numbers, symbols and crystals to name a few. Below are 2 practices to help you clear your energy matrix to help you find your still point to quieting the mind. Use what feels right for you and leave what doesn't. Play with your practice and you are encouraged to experiment. Hold your intent with purpose throughout the practices and come back to it until it appears in physical form for the best results.

Rituals
Clearing & Releasing- Waning Moon
Restoring & Rejuvenating-Waxing Moon
Amplifying & Expanding-Full Moon

There is at least a 3 day window you can use around each time of the month for your rituals.

Shower or bathe with Himalayan, Celtic, or any salt that still have its mineral content.

Create your own customized Quiet Mind Tea Blend using the herbs: Lemon Balm(Melissa), Chamomile, Passion Flower, Gotu Kola, Lavender, Valerian, Nettles, Kava Kava and Ginkgo Biloba. These are only a few to get you started in the adventure. If tea is not your thing, you can use the powdered herb in veggie capsule form as well or take tincture blend.

Apply, diffuse and or spritz you favorite essential oil blend that works with the ritual you are doing. For example, to amplify and expand my energies for clearer intuition and insight in the full moon phase, I can use Clary Sage, Lemongrass or Frankincense. I can also combined them into a blend to create a new synergy blend that offers benefits of all three oils. If you want to get to know your oils

more intimately, I would start with one oil at a time first until you're more familiar with the personality traits of that particular oil. You will then be more aware of what oil to use in your rituals for specific results.

Add water safe crystals like Clear Quartz, Amethyst, Moonstone or Smoky Quartz to your bath & drinking water to raise the frequencies of your water.

Play frequencies or tuning fork that resets the body and auric field. Here are some to get you started. I use these regularly and notice when I have not been tuning my energetic field.

When you play these frequencies while in water, it is said to be at least five times as effective than with out since water is the perfect substance to transmit sound and we are at least 70% water as adults. When we submerse our body in water it amplifies the effect of sound being able to traveling through the body and going where it's need.

174Hz-Helps to take pain out of the body. It can relieve tension and rewire the energy of the brain to experience more positive emotions

136.1 Hz -Called Ohm or Mid Ohm, it is the sound of creation. It helps to release stress on the heart It's my favorite fork and weighted. It totally soothes me with in minutes.

417Hz -helps with emotional issues & clears negative energy. Use it throughout your home to clear the space.

528Hz -Known as the love frequency, miracle tone or frequency of transformation. It repairs DNA and rejuvenates.

These frequencies can be found online easily. I suggest at least a 30 minute session guided by your intuition. Your meditations will become easier using this process.

Meditation - Use alone or after ritual

This meditation can be done anywhere or anytime as long as you can smile, feel relaxed in all parts of your body and focus inward without being disturbed.

Instead of focusing on sitting a specific way and moving as little as possible, the goal is to just make sure that your spine is erect, your head is lifted off of your neck and you can feel your breath move through your body. This can be sitting up, lying down or standing.

If you need a focus point, you can use a candle. Good colors for quieting the mind are blues, purples and white.

Crystals or Gemstones like Clear Quartz, Lapis Lazuli, Angelite, Amethyst can also clear the auric field of debris and energetic dissonance

To find your zone faster, you can use an essential oil like Frankincense or Sandalwood that can

If smoke is your thing you can also still the mind with Palo Santo for stress, anxiety and depression.

See if you can slow your breath to about 6 breaths per minute.

In your breaths envision the colors, all shades of blues, purples and white

Think of something that makes you happy. Smile as wide as you can. Breathe slowly into that thought. Hold on to a happy image, feel yourself enjoying the moment. Let that feeling flow through your body Some may prefer to focus on a mantra or mantram like Ra Ma or Om Mani Padme Hum. This can help you to eventually move sound more freely through your body. It can also help open the 5th chakra area related to the throat. This will allow you to express your truth easier and communicate more lovingly with others. You can say your favorite mantra or mantram silently or out loud.

Both ways are effective.

Some like to hold a sigil with symbolism that is important to them in the mind to anchor their attention.

I find all ways work and I combine a few as needed. I allow my intuition to tell me what to include in each particular meditation session. It's all good if it feels good for your practice.

Close your eyes lightly, pull the head off of the neck through the center of the head & allow the body to totally relax. Envision your are in a vast ocean of different shades of blues and whites surrounding you from head to toe. You are submersed in the cosmic ocean. As you smile, you let the waves sway you as you focus on where your breath is in your body. When thoughts take over you and you feel like your losing consciousness of where your breath is, return to it with a smile and keep letting go while following your breath and letting it go where it wants to.

Allow 30 minutes or longer for your meditation if you can. If 30 minutes is all you have meditate for 20 minutes and use 10 minutes to slowly return to daily life by calling all parts of your self from all time lines, dimensions and realities back to the current moment. Stretch

the body in ways that are comfortable for you. You may experience the urge to yarn, stretch, twist your body slowly, roll your neck or stick your tongue out while you are letting the waves of the cosmic ocean carry you. This is part of the letting go process.

Pam Swing

Writer-Artist. Grandmother. Seeker.

Pam Swing, Ph.D. facilitates sacred circles of women who are in transition and wish to deepen their inner journey. Her work with women grows out of her association with the former Greenfire Women's Retreat in Maine. She was also trained as a SoulCollage® facilitator by founder Seena Frost. Through SoulCollage® and other expressive practices, she helps women recognize and cultivate the conditions that foster renewal and growth. An accomplished photographer, Pam has been exhibiting her feminine images of nature and other photographs since 1997. She is currently on sabbatical from her circle work while completing a manuscript for a creative nonfiction book about her suffragist grandmother, Betty Gram Swing.

www.BlueMoonCreativity.com

Conjunction

Under the light of a half moon,
in the snow-covered field behind our house,
I stamp out the twists and turns
of a seven-coil labyrinth.

In the dark western sky,
Jupiter and Saturn
give each other a high five
as their orbits swing them into a stately do-si-do.

It is a unique moment, this alignment of
labyrinth making and planetary caress.

Saturn and Jupiter,
who take the long view on things,
can look forward to greeting each other again
in sixty years.

I will be long gone.

I trace the ancient sacred pattern
and retrace my steps with vigor.
The trajectory of my orbit becomes visible,
like Venus appearing in the evening sky.

Not perfect, but good enough.

Blue Moon Yurt - Labyrinth from front August 2018:

Pam's Conjunction Snow Labyrinth 2020:

Patricia Diorio

Spiritual Mentor. Sacred Storyteller.
Professional Intuitive.

Patricia Diorio, M.S. has a private counseling practice in Santa Barbara, CA. She is a Transformational Speaker & Sacred Storyteller who is committed to informing, inspiring and motivating people to achieve their goals and dreams through raising consciousness by deepening spiritual awareness. In her early career as a social worker administrator, she directed two high profile non-profit organizations — Big Brothers/Big Sisters and Catholic Charities. Later, she was the creator, producer and host of two TV series *The Paradigm Shift* and *Get Conscious Now!* Over the years, she has produced 335 shows in Santa Barbara on the connection between science and spirituality highlighting the recent discoveries in quantum physics. Her guests have included such renown scholars as Dr. Deepak Chopra, Dr. Bruce Lipton, and Dr. Joe Dispenza. The greatest takeaway from her media work is that science and spirituality are the same conversation from different perspectives.

www.PatriciaDiorio.com

Paradigm Shift...
It's Happening Now

"You're such a Pollyanna, Trishie" my mother laughingly used to tell me. I remember feeling at the time that it was not a compliment, but rather a subtle or "cute" way to criticize my idealism, which I'm sure occurred to my mother as gullibility, innocence and vulnerability. I think she worried about this tendency in my life from early childhood.

Today, having lived over 7 decades devoted to finding and living my life purpose, I know that what my mother called a "pollyanna," I call a "cosmic optimist and a visionary."

And so, I say without hesitation, that I'm very excited about this unprecedented time in the history of humanity because I believe and I would even go so far as saying that I have a knowing, that we are on the brink of global change for the better.

Twenty four years ago, I began a TV show in Santa Barbara on cable called *The Paradigm Shift*. The purpose of the program was to demonstrate the connection between science and spirituality, which I theorized were the same conversation.

I emphasized the concept of unity consciousness and the interconnectedness of all life everywhere, that

there is no separation. I chose the title *The Paradigm Shift*, and I knew I was in trouble when one of my crew asked me what a *par a ∂ig um* was.

Nevertheless, I kept the title, the implication being that there was a huge shift in consciousness that was taking place on the planet that would eventually result in the awakening of humanity. Awakening to what, you might ask? To the idea that we are all energy beings in physical forms, spiritual beings having a human experience. When I say this I am not making any religious allusions. My focus has been and still is science and spirituality.

And so, on the other side of this paradigm shift, I see science catching up with consciousness. I see science providing irrefutable, irrevocable evidence to the fact that we are all divine beings living in a third dimension reality, having a human experience. And moreover, that everything in existence is of that divine source, as well. Everybody and everything inextricably interconnected in the web of life, no matter who or what. This is Unity Consciousness.

I recently heard one of my favorite teachers and scientists, Dr. Bruce Lipton, the author of *The Biology of Belief*, present his take on the Coronavirus. He said that he was actually excited, like I am, and was almost feeling guilty because he was celebrating this event.

He explained with the perfect metaphor:

He likened humanity to the caterpillar, which destroys its environment by munching every leaf of the milk weed plant, stripping it naked. Then it retreats into the chrysalis where it begins complete breakdown resulting in an elixir of mush that we all know magically transforms into the Monarch Butterfly...beautiful, peaceful and free.

Humanity is in breakdown mode now. The dire political climate, and Covid19, are the catalysts that are expediting this breakdown. I think we all knew major change was needed and inevitable.

What if... this change is happening now? What if this change is the paradigm shift that so many of us have been talking about for so long? I feel very positive and encouraged this is so, and that on the other side of all this mayhem and suffering is a new normal based on acceptance of all people, a balanced economy, healthcare for all, world peace and most of all knowing our true nature as divine.

Yes, we are on the brink of major transformation collectively as the paradigm shifts, and we are also going through our own personal shifts. I would even venture to say that you who are reading this are in the midst of your own personal paradigm shifts. True? True!

Well, I'm right there with you. My personal shift has been expedited by a new body of work that came into my life on my 70th birthday in 2015. I had been doing spiritual counseling for 20 years, helping people connect with their Essence, their True Selves deepening their spiritual awareness. Now, it felt like I needed to deepen my mine. So, on my 75th birthday, I brazenly shook my fist at God, (metaphorically, of course) and said "Hey, Darling, what about me? What's next for me to take a deeper dive? I'm ready. Show me!"

That very afternoon a good friend and spiritual colleague said, "Patricia, you have to get this book. I think you will love it. It's called *I Am The Word* by Paul Selig." Just hearing the name stirred something deep in my solar plexus. It was almost like an ache, a yearning. I paid attention and called the local metaphysical book store. Surprisingly, they had never heard of it. I ordered it and I will never forget the day I picked it up. As I held the book in my hands, I could have sworn I could feel it vibrating. I felt the energy and it was almost exhilarating. I was excited. In fact, I can't remember ever feeling as excited about reading a book as I did with this one.

Reading *I Am The Word* was like quenching my thirst for finding God. I couldn't get enough of it. In the first year. I read the book three times cover to cover. The authors, working with Paul as the conscious channel for their teaching, identify themselves as Master Teachers, non physical beings who have taken on the assignment of helping humanity transition during this tumultuous time on the planet. They are our Guides and their message is simple and clear.

We are God in human form. They go on to say that everyone is, even the so called bad guys whom we so easily vilify. In fact, they tell us that "We cannot not be God" and that true atheism is not accepting ourselves as such.

What I find particularly exciting is that the Guides have brought the concept of frequency keenly into my awareness. I have always loved how science is the wind under the wings of spirituality, doing its best to decipher the mystery of consciousness, and that is an ongoing process. Inspired by reading the *Word* books, I have done considerable work researching frequency and now I have an understanding that makes so much sense. I believe that frequency is the language of the Universe, not English! Why? Well, because Quantum Physics says that everyone and everything in existence is energy vibrating at a frequency that determines its density. We are energy beings vibrating at our own personal frequency. Who knew? The thing is that when we are stuck in negative thinking, which is always fueled by fear, we vibrate at a low frequency. When we are being present to our thoughts and consciously choose them and keep them positive, we are vibrating at a high frequency.

The Guides are committed to raising our frequency while we are in the body helping us sustain a higher and higher vibration. They call this ascension. They are gradually lifting our frequency and catalyzing our ascension while we are in the body. We're talking physiological changes here. Wow! Think about that for moment. I find it mind blowing.

When we hear the word ascension, I would guess that most people think that ascension happens after we die or, as I like to say, after we drop the body. The Guides tell us that ascension is happening now for all humanity, commensurate with a person's level of consciousness. They say their *Word* work is the vehicle they offer for those who are game and ready to take a very deep dive. That would be me. However, they also make a point of saying that there are many paths on the planet at this time that are also assisting in the ascension process.

I feel fortunate to have found this one and I have an unshakable trust in their every word. A fact I find rather astounding is that all the books are completely unedited per the Guides' request. This is because every word carries the vibrational intention of what they are teaching. Even if Paul mis-heard a word, they do not want it corrected in the publishing.

I am living testimony of this efficacy of this Book and of this *Word* work. I am not the same person I was when I started this endeavor over 6 years ago. Now 8 books later, I know I am vibrating at a higher frequency. I can feel it. My perception of the world has changed and therefore my life has changed... for the better. Due to a generous patron who came to me about a year into the *Work*, I've been given the amazing opportunity to expand my career as a Transformational Speaker and Sacred Storyteller.

This is so exciting! It's what I've been waiting for. It's why I came.

Gosh! This piece of writing sounds like an infomercial for the Book and I've certainly been on my soap box. However, I won't apologize because if I've inspired you enough to check it out, that's reward enough for me.

One last share...up to the the time the book came into my life, including 25 years of spiritual counseling, and 335 television shows on science and spirituality, I believed that we were divine beings, each of us a unique expression of God, or whatever name you want to use. Today I don't just believe it...**I know it.**

Patricia's passion is helping people deepen their understanding of spirituality and what it means to live life consciously. Her vision is to inspire humanity to awaken to the Truth that we are Spiritual Beings having a human experience with innate power to create our reality personally and collectively. Her mission is to communicate, collaborate and co-create with like minded thought leaders to raise the consciousness of Humanity.

Sloane Reali

Warrior. Leader. Healer.

Sloane Reali has been a Voice and Confidence Coach for over 20 years helping public speakers, teachers, therapists, doctors and authors to prepare vocally in their professions. A leader in her field making guest appearances on Television and Radio as an expert on the power of voice, clients have used Sloane's services to prepare for auditions including American Idol, The Voice, and Disney. Others have started their own bands, writing and publishing their own music, and making guest appearances with music royalty such as David Foster, Lionel Richie and Stevie Wonder to name a few. Sloane splits her time between Hollywood, Santa Barbara and Paso Robles, CA with her husband and 3 kids. She has found the practice of Ayurveda to be helpful for balancing a full life, eating and sleeping according to her doshas, and daily meditation vital to staying centered in order to fully show up for those she serves.

www.VocalCoachingBySloane.com

Breathing Your Way to Balance
(Using your Voice)

My story really begins with what I do today professionally as an Expert Voice and Confidence Coach serving women who need help finding and accessing their voice so they feel heard and supported in their personal lives, validated and respected in their professional lives. A literal transformation in confidence takes place when using simple and effective tools while creating new habits and beliefs about our value and our worth. It's part "how to" but also a journey of personal, emotional and most exciting - physical healing.

Breathing is something I've struggled with from birth, experiencing my first asthma attack at six months old. This was followed by regular visits to emergency rooms, where I was given steroids to open my airway and hooked to ventilators to help me breathe. This continued well into my childhood spending many birthdays and an occasional Christmas in the hospital recovering from pneumonia. I remember feeling awful after being medicated and disliked the anxiety the medication would cause so intensely that when I would feel an asthma attack coming on, I taught myself, as a small child, to slow my breathing and heart rate down to a slower pace. Somehow, either through meditation or visualization, (I didn't know what these modalities were yet), I could prevent a full blown attack bypassing the meds. Not realizing what I was doing at such a young age - it's become clear this is the very thing I now help others to do.

One particularly frightening memory is when I was seven years old. I woke in the middle of the night with yet another asthma attack and what smelled like my mother had left an empty coffee pot on the burner. You know that smell of burnt coffee? I left the bedroom I shared with my little sister who was five. When I entered the hallway it was filled with flames. Half asleep and in a panic I woke my parents who still had to get my baby brother from the room closest to the flames. I recall fleeing for our lives out the master bedroom window. I remember the sirens, the lights, the moist night air smell. It was fall. The fire was arson. We never did find out who tried to do away with me and my family. There was always some sort of drama going on. If there was any blessing in me having upper respiratory challenges...this was it. I remember seeing the newspaper headline. *"Family Flees Flames" saved by second grader* - that was me. Investigators said had we not woken up we would surely have perished by smoke inhalation. My parakeets in the garage were not so lucky.

When I began teaching voice over two decades ago, it truly was about teaching people how to sing. What shifted were people started reaching out to me not so much for singing but rather for speaking

and presenting with confidence. I began to receive clients who were prescribed vocal coaching from their Ear-Nose-Throat Doctors, their Pulmonologists and Speech Therapists. Stroke and cancer survivors, people with brain injuries and surgeries of the throat that didn't go as planned, even the hearing impaired found their way to me and have all benefitted from voice coaching. Voice challenges continue to rise exponentially given the increase in people working remotely and the use of protective masks which make it even more difficult to be heard - literally!

It's worth noting that upper respiratory challenges are located in the heart/lung area of the body and also associated with grief, loss, trauma - which is part of my experience as a spiritual being having a physical experience on the planet at this time in history. We know stress contributes to all sorts of imbalances in the body. These aren't just physical. They're mental and emotional as well. In fact, individuals who struggle with these types of issues are often told or believe they're imagining it, or told "it's all in your head." I'm here to tell you, listen to your body and trust your gut, your higher intuition. We have the capacity to heal ourselves on so many levels.

As I write, I'm grateful beyond words that I no longer struggle with any type of upper respiratory issues and many of the health concerns I did as a child and into adulthood. I'm currently healthier than I've ever been in my entire life. I've taken note of the years of medical treatments and non-traditional therapies

along with eastern medicine, bio-feedback and even an out of body experience with a Shaman.

We commonly think what ails us is outside of us, when really it starts inside the body and the mind. Our perspective and attitude have everything to do with how we show up in the world, how we're treated and how we treat others starting with ourselves. I continue to practice daily meditation, breathwork and visualization to maintain a balanced life. I listen to and honor my body paying attention to the signs when something's not right or causing me stress.

I never imagined that having a potentially life threatening illness as a child could bring me to a place of such powerful healing not just for myself but for those I love and serve. The journey is not over as I apply these same principles to other areas in my life. I'm reminded that this work was not just for me but rather for me to share with others. This is one of my many contributions to making the planet a better place - a place of peace and love, acceptance and forgiveness, for ourselves, for others and for those to come.

"Our deepest fear is not that we are inadequate.
Our deepest fear is that
we are powerful beyond measure..."
- Marianne Williamson, from *A Return to Love*

Tam Veilleux

Visionary. Artist. Coach.

Tam Veilleux is the lead visionary of the Energy Almanac. As an author, artist and coach, her passion is for helping people who are stuck to connect the dots and shine bright, feel good, and grow to their greatest version of themselves through astrology, energy psychology and illustrated products and services. She feels that too many entrepreneurs avoid doing the hard work of seeking out blocks. Her approach is to ask the tough questions and look for answers in the natal birth chart. Tam is a cosmic chocolate covered pretzel acting as a transformational coach by day and astrology student by night. She offers visual chatter via social media on the alchemy and strategy of creating change.

www.TheEnergyAlmanac.com

Review, Reflect, Renew
for Clarity and Confidence

Ahhh, the waning gibbous moon! Under the light of the waning full moon you have the perfect opportunity to bring a new kind of clarity to your life. The value of a thorough review must not be understated.

In my practice as a transformational life coach I encourage my audience to sit down, take a breath, and look back at what might bring them forward. It is by looking for gaps and missteps in what we've done, how we felt about it, and the performance results that provide a better roadmap for the days, weeks, and months ahead.

If you're paying attention to a lunar cycle, then you may already know the sweet starts that happen under the New Moon each month. And you're probably familiar with the releasing period of the Full Moon as well. But what happens in between those two celebrated lunations can have just as much value.

The dark of the New Moon is when we first set eyes on what we are growing for the next 28.5 days. The waxing period that follows is a time to take certain steps toward amplifying the hoped-for result. It's a time of sowing seeds, watering, and cultivating.

At the Full Moon we contemplate, "What might be in the way of the best outcome?" Release is the key word for that mid-way moon. The days between Full and New Moons are the waning moons. And it's under the waning gibbous that we can truly review actions and emotions, reflect on how we can change, and then renew our enthusiasm for attaining the goal set under the New Moon, or change course completely.

Life is sure busy and perhaps marking your calendar with the waning gibbous moon isn't a practical matter for you. As a stand-in, try a month end review.

How to do a month-end review:

Grab a pencil and a notebook, find a quiet spot and ask the question: *Did you hit your goal?* If you did, then immediately write at the top of the page in big letters, "HELL YES I hit my goal!"

Focus Word. What was the focus word for the month you just went through? (Hopefully you chose one at the beginning of the new month under the New Moon.) How did you do with that word? Reflect on it. Was it powerful for you? Did you slip? Write a sentence or two about the meaning of that word in the previous month. Was it valuable for you? Make a note about some potential words for the month ahead.

Life Areas. There are five major life areas worth considering: time, money, health, relationships, spirituality. Write these titles down on your paper and consider each of them carefully. How did you do? Was your time well spent or wasted away? Did you manage your money especially well? Is your health vibrant and strong or weak and lacking? How did you show up inside of relationships? Is your spiritual health in tact?

All of these questions should be considered. Make careful notes about any changes that occurred over the previous time period. Decide where adjustments can be made.

Wins. Look at the things that went right during the month. Hopefully, you have created a list of them in your journal. List at least three of your favorite things that happened during the previous thirty days. Smile as you list them! Go a step further, share your celebrations with someone who loves you. It feels good to voice our accomplishments aloud.

Compliments. Who said what to you? Think back to what you've been doing and who you've bumped into. Search your brain for someone who complimented your work ethic, your smile, your new program, the way you dance, how you cook. Find something that stands out and write the compliment out and put their name next to it. Ahhh, it feels nice, doesn't it? You are rewarded just for being you! Draw lots of stars and hearts around the compliments you wrote down.

Wishes. This is an area for you to write your thoughts about things you'd like to happen in the upcoming 30 days. Perhaps you wish to self-correct in a life area. Maybe you hit your money goal and need to increase it. Maybe there is an energy you want to play with. Whatever it may be, write a wish or two that you will work toward for the next month.

Magic Moments. Collecting magic moments will be the best thing you do this year. Looking back at the previous thirty days, connect the dots backwards. See where something entered your life that you yourself did not coordinate. Sure you may be the one who planned to attend the party, but were you the one that coordinated having that handsome engineer there. The same handsome engineer that you had coffee with to discuss your home's new addition? The same handsome engineer who then invited you to dinner? Write a note about that unexpected "thing" that created momentum for you. These kinds of things are magic and are provided as gifts to you from the Multi-verse. Look for ways that magic entered into your days, acknowledge them joyfully and expect to get more. Feel free to draw a smiley face around your Magic Moments section.

After the review:

With the review, reflect process complete, it's time to renew your desires and goals. Open a new page in your journal and write the name of the month ahead of

you. If you're reviewing October, then the next page will be titled November:

- First, write the name of the upcoming month in the big banner.

- In the upper right corner in the banner, write a focus word that will help lead you through the upcoming 30 days. Use a sticky note to write that focus word again. Stick that note onto the first week of your weekly planner pages and keep transferring it week by week.

- Enter goals into the new page for the month ahead.

Now, take a deep breath and look at your goal that you may have determined for the year or perhaps just for the quarter. Be really in tune with your body as you look at your goals. Do they amplify your energy as you read them or upset your tummy? How is the progress looking? If you've made progress and are on track, pat yourself on the back. If you need to add some tasks into your weekly planning, do that. Maybe you just need to check in with your heart, is this a desire you truly want or are you going for it because someone else thinks you should?

Handwrite your goal(s) in sentence form adding some cool, juicy, titillating details if the goals are truly what you desire. If not, revamp them and adjust your tasks in your day planner. You're onto great things

this year. Keep on keeping on.

Go next level, right now go to your planner and block off an afternoon for next month's review process.

Waning moon or a sun shiny day, what matters the most is that you honor the need to look back so that you may propel yourself forward. It is through a thorough review that the best of ourselves is revealed.

Women of Spirit, Sacred Paths of Wisdom Keepers

is the first volume of this series. It is a compilation of women sojourners, sages, mystics, witches, shaman, medicine women, ministers, philosophers, therapists, life coaches, yogis, and more.
Their journeys.
Their stories.
Their teachings and practices. Essays, Poetry, Art, Rituals and Prayers. This anthology is full of useful tools and powerful messages for everyone who is on a spiritual journey to embrace and enjoy.
Beloved Contributors include:

• *Anna Huckabee Tull* •
• *Bernadette Rombough* •
• *Deborah Diamond* • *Debra Wilson Guttas* • *Grace Ventura* •
• *Janeen Barnett* • *JoAnne Bassett* • *Judy Ann Foster* • *Julie Matheson* •
• *Kate Early* • *Kate Kavanagh* • *Katherine Glass* • *Kris Oster* •
• *Lea M. Hill* • *Meghan Gilroy* • *Morwen Two Feathers* •
• *Rustie MacDonald* • *Shamanaca* • *Sharon Hinckley* • *Shawna Allard*
•• *Shiloh Sophia* • *Susan Feathers* • *Tiffany Cano* • *Tory Londergan* •
"Twinkle" Marie Manning •
• *Tziporah Kingsbury* • *Valerie Sorrentino* •

www.MatrikaPress.com/women-of-spirit

Image caption (on cover):
Women of Spirit
Exploring Sacred Paths of Wisdom Keepers
Compiled and Edited by "Twinkle" Marie Manning
Cover Art by Shiloh Sophia
a Sojourn With Light Workers book

Book Discussion Groups

Many have found that Matrika Press Books are ideal for Book Discussion Groups. The *Women of Spirit* original series covers many diverse perspectives on the topic of exploring sacred paths of key modern-day wisdom keepers. The second book in the *Women of Spirit* series dives into aspects of transformation unique to each contributor. As a collection, or with the subtitles of each contributed chapter as a singular focus, the content of the *Women of Spirit* anthologies make for insightful conversations during women's book study groups. Likewise with other books published by Matrika Press. On the pages that follow, there are outlines for several books Matrika Press has published by "Twinkle" Marie Manning which are wonderful for individual contemplation and group study alike, including her Blessing Book series.

Should your group wish to schedule one of our contributing authors to speak at your gathering or event, please email:

Editor@MatrikaPress.com

ABOUT
Matrika Press

Matrika Press is an independent publishing house dedicated to publishing works in alignment with transformational religious and spiritual values and principles.

Matrika Press has published anthologies, memoirs, poetry, prayer and ritual manuscripts, and other books to bring meaning and transformation to the world. A primary goal of Matrika Press is to publish stories and works that would otherwise remain untold. We also resurrect out-of-print manuscripts to ensure our historical works remain accessible and publish transformational fiction for a small number of authors.

Beginning in 2021, with the exception of fulfilling contracts with existing clients, we will be focusing almost exclusively on publishing:

- Anthologies;
- Anthology Series;
and our
- Pocketful Books.

We have found that this is our niche. We are also seeking co-curators for the *Women of Spirit* series.

For information about how to collaborate on the *Women of Spirit* series or any anthology as a method of outreach and fundraising for your organization, congregation, business or group, email:

Editor@MatrikaPress.com

Why the name "Matrika"?

It is said that Matrika is the intrinsic energy or sound vibration of the 50 letters of the Sanskrit alphabet called "the mothers of creation." The Goddess Kali Ma used the letters to form words, and from the words formed all things. This aligns with scriptures that assert "in the beginning was the Word," and in other sacred texts that affirm people of all backgrounds and faiths agree: Words are powerful. More than that: Their vibrations are creative forces; they bring all things into being.

Matrika Press titles are automatically made available to tens of thousands of retailers, libraries, schools, and other distribution and fulfillment partners, including Amazon, Barnes & Noble, Chapters/Indigo (Canada), and other well-known book retailers and wholesalers across North America, and in the United Kingdom, Europe, Australia and New Zealand and other Global partners.

For more information, visit:

www.MatrikaPress.com

BLESSING BOOK SERIES

Uniquely designed to be journals, spiritual exploration tools and self-led retreats, *Blessing Books* can be used to mark a milestone such as a significant birthday or important season of your life. *Blessing Books* can help you process a loss or transition. It can be where you express your gratitude or your grief. It can be the place you affirm what is next for you as you cross a threshold and visualize your greatest intention for your life. Essentially, *Blessing Books* are where you can contemplate and document your inner-most thoughts, feelings, beliefs and experiences.

Wherever you are on your journey, and in both times of joy and in times of sorrow, may these books serve you well.

For additional *Blessing Book* themes and meditation tools, visit:

www.MatrikaPress.com/blessing-books

www.MatrikaPress.com/family-blessing-book

www.MatrikaPress.com/30-days-of-reflection

Blue Christmas,
*A Guided Retreat to Ease Your Heartache
and Bring Peace of Mind*

Holding your grief sacred during this holiday
season. This Blue Christmas book is designed
to be used as a self-led retreat to guide you
during your quiet reflective moments
this holiday season. It is where you can
contemplate and document your inner-most
thoughts, feelings and beliefs.

Holidays can be emotional and challenging
times laden with sadness, worry and fear.
Stress and heartache, especially grief, are often
amplified. The holidays, while filled with light,
can create palpable darkness.

This *Blue Christmas* book is where you can hold
your grief sacred throughout the holiday season.

www.MatrikaPress.com/blue-christmas

www.MatrikaPress.com/moosehead-lake-reflections

Matrika Press is accepting submissions from authors and artists who wish to collaborate on theme-based and location-based *Blessing Book* series. Our blessing books are often in the form of guided journals containing quotes, mantras and prompts. They can also be ritual, prayer, and meditation-style books.

Should you wish to collaborate, email:

Editor@MatrikaPress.com

Divinely inspired.
Practically written.

Living Life as a Prayer
presents a transformational theology that is
accessible to everyone who wishes to embrace
life in gratitude and grace.

As a spiritual guidebook,
Living Life as a Prayer outlines
principles and practices to help us
more deeply connect with that which we
personally and uniquely identify as holy.

*In her seminal work, Rev. Porter-Manning
shepherds readers toward realizing our intrinsic
connection to each other, and to the Divine.*

www.MatrikaPress.com/twinkle-marie-manning

Poetry by
"Twinkle" Marie Porter-Manning

"Twinkle" Marie Porter-Manning's writings
have been included in publications
and services around the world.
For the first time bound in a poetry book
all their own, her selected writings,
some mystic in nature,
others raw with physical-world portrayals
of the landscapes we live in,
created with passion, emotion,
reflection and thoughtfulness.

Throughout, it is clear she recognizes our journeys
are *Accompanied* with those who weave
in and out of our lives: the people,
the places, the creatures.

Upon reading, one quickly realizes that,
even in mundane things,
the Divine is right there too.

A compelling collection
worthy of contemporary exploration.

www.MatrikaPress.com/Accompanied

Authors
Television
Series

Empowering
W O M E N

For Your Soul

and Featured
Female Leaders

www.EmpoweringWomenTV.org

To join the Empowering Women Team,
Host a Salon Gathering or Signature Event,
to be a Guest,
and for Sponsor inquiries, email:
EmpoweringWomenTelevision@gmail.com

CPSIA information can be obtained
at www.ICGtesting.com
Printed in the USA
JSHW012033030822
28864JS00007B/211